Praise for *The Money Coach's Guide to Your First Million*

"*The Money Coach's Guide to Your First Million* will make you financially healthy, wealthy, and wise. Its seven-step plan is worth its weight in gold."

> Tavis Smiley
> Author, Television & Radio Host

"Lynnette Khalfani's *The Money Coach's Guide to Your First Million* is compelling for wanna-be millionaires, making you a millionaire-in-training upon opening the cover! It gives you basics for getting your house in order from which to launch your financial future. Anyone can get started toward financial freedom with this book."

> Kenneth L. Fisher
> Founder and CEO, Fisher Investments and
> 22-year *Forbes* "Portfolio Strategy" columnist

"Just starting out in the world of money? Khalfani's patient and prudent approach is the kick in the pants you need to get on the road toward financial freedom. Her decidedly old-school take on building wealth combines Depression-era frugality with a contemporary, no-nonsense style. Unlike the get-rich-quick schemes that now infest popular financial literature, the lessons presented in this book will never go out of style."

> Jonathan Hoenig
> Portfolio Manager, Capitalistpig Hedge Fund LLC
> and Fox News Channel personality

"Lynnette Khalfani has written a great little book with many gems to guide you toward your first million. It's got terrific material on planning, paying down your debt, understanding real estate investments, and even how to avoid the obstacles that could kill off your efforts. It's a seven-step plan that will point you in the right direction."

> Dr. Van K. Tharp
> Trading Coach and author of the *NY Times* Best
> Seller, *Safe Strategies for Financial Freedom*

"Money Coach Lynnette Khalfani shares the secrets of the rich, and shows you exactly how you too can join the millionaires' club. If you dream of one day owning your own business, you'll especially love this book's wisdom on how entrepreneurship builds wealth."

> Dr. Randal Pinkett, Founder and CEO, BCT Partners
> *The Apprentice*, Season 4 with Donald Trump

The Money Coach's Guide to
YOUR FIRST MILLION

---

7 Smart
Habits to
Building the
Wealth of
Your Dreams

LYNNETTE KHALFANI

McGraw-Hill

NEW YORK | CHICAGO | SAN FRANCISCO | LISBON
LONDON | MADRID | MEXICO CITY | MILAN | NEW DELHI
SAN JUAN | SEOUL | SINGAPORE | SYDNEY | TORONTO

The **McGraw·Hill** Companies

1 2 3 4 5 6 7 8 9 0 DOC/DOC 0 10 9 8 7

ISBN-13: 978-0-07-147081-0
ISBN-10: 0-07-147081-6

McGraw-Hill books are available at special quantity discounts to use as premiums and sales promotions, or for use in corporate training programs. For more information, please write to the Director of Special Sales, Professional Publishing, McGraw-Hill, Two Penn Plaza, New York, NY 10121-2298. Or contact your local bookstore.

This book is printed on recycled, acid-free paper containing a minimum of 50% recycled, de-inked fiber.

Library of Congress Cataloging-in-Publication Data

Khalfani, Lynnette.
 The money coach's guide to your first million / by Lynnette Khalfani.
  p. cm.
 ISBN 0-07-147081-6 (alk. paper)
 1. Finance, Personal. 2. Investments. 3. Financial security I. Title.
HG179.K43 2007
332.024'01—dc22

2006021202

To my children: Aziza, Jakada, and Alexis.

You represent the best of me

and the promise of the next generation.

T his book would never have seen the light of day were it not for a fabulous group of people who all worked together to make *The Money Coach's Guide to Your First Million* the product you now hold.

First and foremost, special thanks to Earl Cox, my agent, manager, and all-around life partner. Somehow "thank you" seems woefully inadequate for all that you do. When I look back at the last year and a half, I marvel at how we made it through so many transitions—personally and professionally. In you I've found a rare combination: a loving mate who always puts my best interests first, a best friend who supports me at every turn, and a business collaborator who does everything humanly possible to take my career to the next level. I love you too, Earl, and am eternally grateful for your kindness and the many blessings you've brought into my life.

Deborah Darrell, of Cue, you remain a source of inspiration, constantly raising the bar and forcing me to "always bring my 'A' game." Don't ever think you're being too hard on me. You know how to say what needs to be said—tactfully, artfully or just straight-out, if necessary. I need a coach like you to keep me striving for the best.

To my editor, Jeanne Glasser, and the entire team at McGraw-Hill, I know it's not easy working with authors. We can be such a demanding group, and I'm no exception. That's why I truly appreciate your efforts.

To Anthony Barboza, photographer extraordinaire, my heartfelt thanks for capturing me at my best—and just a few months after the birth of my little one! Your work is amazing.

I would be remiss if I did not acknowledge everyone who agreed to be interviewed for this book. You are too numerous to mention by name, but just know that I'm genuinely grateful for your time, expertise, and opinions.

Last, but certainly not least, many thanks to my coaching clients and the thousands of people who attended my workshops and seminars over the years. You often remarked about how much you learned in our sessions. The truth is that by sharing your stories with me—whether those tales were triumphs or tragedies—you taught me a great deal about how people of all ages, races, backgrounds, incomes, and professions have a fundamental need for financial security. You also helped me to understand the practical and emotional obstacles to achieving wealth, and why certain conventional wisdom from personal finance "experts" doesn't work in the real world. Please know that your past experiences have prepared you for bigger and better things. Your insights and experiences will also help create a new generation of millionaires.

CONTENTS

INTRODUCTION

E very day nearly 25,000 people in the United States become newly minted millionaires. Wouldn't it be nice to be one of them? Come on, admit it. You'd love to wear the title "millionaire" or even "multi-millionaire" so you can finally feel that life is good, financial stress is virtually nonexistent, and money is plentiful. Right?

Let me paint the complete picture: When you're a millionaire, you don't worry about how you're going to pay the rent or the mortgage. When you're a millionaire, bill collectors don't call and harass you. You don't feel like you're living from paycheck to paycheck. You're never declined for credit—whether you're paying for dinner in a restaurant, applying for a new MasterCard, or seeking a home equity line. As a legitimate millionaire, you have more than enough income to pay your financial obligations—and you pay them faithfully, on time. You're in control of your money, instead of it controlling you. Best of all, you have complete financial peace of mind; the kind of peace that comes with a seven-figure bank account and a healthy investment portfolio.

As a millionaire, you travel and vacation when and where you want—without fretting over whether you can afford the trip. You smile when you see your kids playing in the backyard or heading off to school because you know that you've provided well for them and have assured your children of a solid financial future. Having plenty of money in your war chest feels nice.

When you're a millionaire, you're in control of your money, instead of it controlling you.

It's no wonder the TV show *Who Wants to Be a Millionaire?* was so popular. The question is, who *doesn't* want to be a millionaire?

Millionaire Households on the Rise

The great news is that becoming a millionaire isn't a pipe dream. It's within your reach—it's attainable. There are currently unprecedented numbers of millionaires in the United States. According to TNS Financial Services, a market research and polling firm, there were 8.9 million of the 120 million households in the United States with a net worth of at least $1 million in 2005. That's 700,000 more million-dollar households in 2005 than in 2004. And in recent years, the numbers have been steadily rising. So becoming a millionaire isn't as hard to achieve as you might think. Looking at the statistics another way, 8.9 million wealthy households mean that:

- The average American has a 1 in 13 chance of becoming a millionaire.
- Each month, another 741,666 people become millionaires.
- Each week, 171,153 people become millionaires.
- Each day, 24,383 people become millionaires.

So why shouldn't you be one of them?

The Millionaire Success Formula

Whatever your goals and dreams, rest assured that you can achieve them if you have the right regimen and practice good discipline. In this book, I introduce seven universal wealth principles that will guide you as you seek millionaire status. Together these principles make up the Millionaire Success Formula:

M— Make a personal prosperity plan.

Develop a millionaire's budget, written goals, and a Financial Policy Statement.

Establish a regimen for spending, saving, and investing and follow it diligently.

I — Invest first, last, and always in your reputation.

Build perfect credit.

Understand how having a stellar name is often better than having cash in the bank.

L— Live like a lender, not a borrower.

Achieve zero debt.

Decide to collect interest, not pay it, for the rest of your life.

L— Leverage the power of property.

Ramp up with real estate.

Use hard assets and other people's money to build riches.

I — Increase your fortune with proven methods, not shortcuts.

Buy stocks, bonds, and alternative investments when prudent.

Avoid fads, scams and Wall Street long shots.

O — Overcome setbacks and minimize risks to your financial health.

Make insurance a top asset.

Protect yourself against the Dreaded Ds: downsizing, divorce, disability, disease, death in the family, and disaster.

N — Never forget the next generation.

Create wills, trusts, and personal and business succession plans.

Establish a wealth legacy.

I call these *universal* wealth principles for two reasons. First, as The Money Coach, I've had direct contact with tens of thousands of consumers across the country and, based on these dealings, discovered that these wealth principles can be used by anyone—no matter what age, income, race, marital status, or job standing. Second, as a former financial journalist for Dow Jones and a CNBC business news reporter, I have interviewed hundreds of millionaires and thousands of money management experts—everyone from certified financial planners and stockbrokers to CEOs—all of whom either followed these principles to amass wealth or used them with their clients.

The potent combination of implementing all seven principles and the strategies for executing them simultaneously will turn you into a financial powerhouse and enable you to create your own Millionaire Success Formula. Putting these principles into action will help you develop and stick to a concrete, personal plan for creating and maintaining long-term wealth. With this formula, your 1 in 13 chance of becoming a millionaire will improve dramatically. Readers at all levels of personal finance knowledge will deploy each principle one at a time, ultimately combining all seven to become what I like to call a "Millionaire-in-Training."

> **These seven principles in action will help you develop and stick to a concrete, personal plan for creating and maintaining wealth over the long term.**

How To Use This Book

The Money Coach's Guide To Your First Million is divided into seven chapters that mirror the universal wealth principles I describe above; each chapter corresponds to a single step. While I think you'll get the most out of this book by reading it from cover to cover, if there is a certain subject you find of particular interest, you can flip right to that chapter and learn the related strategies, tactics, and ideas that drive that piece of the Millionaire Success Formula.

As your personal Money Coach, I'll share the tips, tricks, and techniques that millionaires have known and practiced for years. In Chapter 1 you'll learn why millionaires love budgets—and how they use them to get even richer. This chapter goes on to explain four simple ways to stop blowing your budget by using proper planning and control. Chapter 2 details a number of little-known methods for creating a stellar credit record that ultimately improves your net worth. I call this The PERFECT CREDIT™ seven-step system. For those of you trying to overcome debt problems, Chapter 3 introduces debt-busting strategies that can wipe out credit card bills, such as sending debt verification letters to collection agents. These letters often legally eliminate debts in their entirety. And if you're one of the 115 million Americans with credit cards, Chapter 3 gives you the low down on how banks and other financial institutions operate. After reading this chapter, you'll be convinced that you need to switch roles and start acting more like a lender than a borrower.

But more importantly, *The Money Coach's Guide To Your First Million* takes you beyond the basics of budgeting, credit, and debt management. With the activity in the housing market, many of you will no doubt be interested in Chapter 4, which describes how to get 30 percent returns without becoming a landlord as well as atypical methods for making money in real estate. And for those of you interested in the stock market, Chapter 5 details the dos and don'ts of investing; in particular, how to avoid losing your shirt on Wall Street. You might be surprised to learn what the top 10 investment scams are today.

Finally, it's not enough to tell you how you're going to get rich. You need to know how to stay that way. So *The Money Coach's Guide To*

Your First Million also reveals the most common ways that millionaires lose their fortunes. You'll want to pay close attention to the six Dreaded Ds: divorce, disability, downsizing, disease, death in the family, and disasters, which include business failures, lawsuits, and money-wasting addictions to drugs or gambling. In Chapters 6 and 7, you'll learn how to safeguard yourself financially against all the Dreaded Ds, and how to creatively use trusts and insurance to avoid these and other pitfalls once you become a millionaire. Chapter 7 also provides you with a vision for the future, explaining why forward-thinking people, who plan not just for years but for generations, are often the richest of all.

> **Each of the seven steps is equally important; you must implement each one if you want to gain lasting material comfort and wealth.**

Again, my goal as your Money Coach is to explain the crucial steps you must take to build enduring wealth, reach millionaire status, and make sure your fortune isn't squandered. Let me emphasize up front that these seven steps are all equally important, and you must tackle each one of them if you want your riches to last a lifetime.

No Get-Rich-Quick Schemes

Some of you may be saying: "Can't I just do *one* thing to become a millionaire?" I wish it were that simple. The reality is that you have to take a multipronged approach in order to gain lasting material comfort and wealth. Just taking one or two steps—or even four or five—won't get you there *and* keep you there. It's the combination of this seven-phase process, all phases working together and guiding you toward your ultimate destination that catapults you to a life of financial freedom.

In case you still need convincing that you absolutely have to work on all seven steps to permanently achieve millionaire status, picture a star basketball player at the height of his game. He's a pro—but he's also a veteran. And, with new players entering the league each year, he knows that he'll probably be around for only a few more seasons at best. For this player, his ultimate dream is to be inducted into the NBA Hall of Fame. To reach that goal, this individual works relentlessly. He's constantly tweaking his defensive and offensive games. He practices free throws for hours at a time, works on his dribbling skills, learns to post up well against bigger competitors, knows when to pass the ball for that all-important assist, and he shoots well from the top of the court too. Ultimately, this player does get into the Hall of Fame. Do you think this would have happened if the player only shot the ball well? Not a chance. It's the merging of all his skills and abilities that helped him reach his goal.

Don't Be Your Own Worst Enemy

Let me also caution you, however, that there are several definite roadblocks to becoming a millionaire. Most are within your power to avoid. However, some are external factors, and you'll have to watch out for those pitfalls too. A few of the obstacles to achieving financial security are discussed below.

LAZINESS

Unfortunately, some people simply aren't willing to work at becoming millionaires. That's a shame because, for many of these individuals, all that stands between them and a lifetime of riches is a lack of drive —call it laziness, if you will. Haven't you ever known someone with great promise and great potential, yet that person never seems to get it together because he or she won't work hard to achieve a goal? Don't let this be your fate. I assume that, by your picking up this book, you're eager to become a millionaire. Promise yourself today that you'll rise to the challenge and maintain the wherewithal required to push you through the process of achieving riches.

PROCRASTINATION

You can't get rich if you put off doing the things necessary to build long-term wealth and maintain your economic security. It's as simple as that. To catapult yourself into the upper echelons of the financial world, you must heed a number of calls. Some of them will require you to start doing things—and immediately. At other times, you'll need to stop doing things. But you won't turn into one of those nearly 25,000 Americans becoming millionaires each day if "I'll do it tomorrow" is your constant mantra. When you learn new information that pushes you to act or if you discover that you need to stop doing something you're currently doing which is taking you off the path to millionaire status, you have to act on that information without delay. Procrastination only inhibits you from reaching your goal. And, by the way, procrastinators come in all different forms: from the 30-something couple who (mistakenly) believes it can put off saving for retirement because it's "so far away, and we have to worry about current bills" to the well-intentioned (but ill-fated) parent who puts off saving for her golden years because she's spending all her money and resources on her children.

PERPETUAL MONEY DRAINERS

I hate to say it, but sometimes, the people in our lives are financial drains in ways that are very unhealthy—a factor that can be a hindrance to someone striving for long-term wealth. In *The Money Coach's Guide To Your First Million*, I'll help you look honestly at the ways in which the people you deal with, the places you go, and the products you spend money on are affecting your ability to become a millionaire.

LACK OF KNOWLEDGE

Ignorance of how to get ahead financially can definitely limit a person's fortunes. And Americans are in desperate need of practical financial advice on everything from how to manage their debt wisely and improve their credit standing to how much insurance they need. The problem is part lack of information and part misinformation. In many instances, though, people are overwhelmed with too much information or just not enough that contains usable advice or realistic recommendations about what to do to solve their problems. One of the objectives of *The Money Coach's Guide To Your First Million* is to act as a bridge for those people who are willing to take action. I give you a concrete plan—a how-to model—to follow that will alleviate financial difficulties and enable you to live a richer life.

NO DISCIPLINE

> **Don't allow laziness, money drainers, procrastination, a lack of knowledge, or a lack of discipline to keep you from becoming a millionaire.**

The person who acquires money isn't always the one who keeps that money, let alone retires wealthy. Consider those high-profile celebrities, athletes and actors, who've earned millions only to wind up in bankruptcy court. In many cases, a lack of discipline in the form of outlandish spending and no fiscal restraint did them in. Chances are you're not a rock and roll star or an NBA player with some multi-million dollar contract. Nevertheless, you still have to exercise discipline and follow-through in a number of areas in order to become and remain a millionaire.

To summarize my point, don't allow laziness, money drainers, procrastination, a lack of knowledge, or a lack of discipline to keep you from becoming a millionaire. Make your commitment to the good life now and decide that nothing, absolutely nothing, will stand in your way.

1

MAKE A PERSONAL PROSPERITY PLAN

I have a confession to make: I'm a financial Dr. Jekyll and Mr. Hyde. That might sound strange coming from someone who's about to tell you how to bank your first million. But it's only right that, probably like you, there are two sides to my personality when it comes to money.

I've amassed great wealth—while at other times I've accumulated tremendous debt. I spent a decade building a six-figure investment portfolio only to fritter it away in a year's time. I didn't blink an eye when I paid $30,000 a year in tuition for my children's education—when they were just three and five years old. But I'd loathe dropping three dollars on a soft drink while dining in a restaurant. So for better or worse, I admit that there's a virtuous side of my money personality and a reckless side as well. Thankfully, the good me wins out far more often than not. That's the part of me that takes pleasure in saving money and watching it grow, and actually enjoys tackling financial chores like doing my taxes or updating my will. Geeky, I know. In other words, that's the Dr. Jekyll in me.

But remember what happened in Robert Louis Stevenson's classic tale? Dr. Jekyll creates a potion that suppresses his good side and lets down his inhibitions. This gives his evil side free rein. And each time Dr. Jekyll drinks the potion, the evil Mr. Hyde grows increasingly powerful, while the normally sensible Dr. Jekyll becomes weaker and more fearful. While Dr. Jekyll ultimately discovers that he can transform himself back from being a fiendish monster by drinking the potion again, his actions raise two interesting questions, namely:

Is there a good side and a dark side lurking in all of us?

Can you control the weaker aspects of your personality once you've indulged them—or will you always be a slave to them?

Royalty Living in Empty Castles

I don't think that I'm alone in battling a split personality when it comes to money. I believe many of us have divided selves with respect to our finances. For instance, the Mr. Hyde in me will allow bills (and paychecks, believe it or not) to go unopened for days. The Hyde part of my personality can relish the thrill of spending like crazy, enjoying what I want in the here and now, and worrying about the financial consequences later. Millions of other Americans do the same thing on a daily basis. I've talked to countless people across the country, mainly middle-class individuals, who've told me in no uncertain terms that they feel like frauds. They are living double lives because they appear to have all the trappings of success, but inwardly they're stressed about bills and barely managing to keep everything afloat. To the outside world, their lives look picture-perfect. In reality, however, they're like royalty living in empty castles. Many times these people can barely sleep at night for fear and worry about how unstable their lives truly are. And often these people, and you may be one of them, are battling their own financial demons. They're earnestly trying to get control of their finances once and for all so that money is not such a big mental drain in their lives.

It's my firm belief that you can manage your money well, without constantly succumbing to your darker impulses—no matter how tempting they may be. There's no magic potion I can conjure to turn your finances around. But I can help you revamp your financial life by having you begin at the beginning; that is, you have to evaluate your current predicament by looking back at how you first came to have certain attitudes and beliefs about money. No matter where you are economically, chances are that much of what you learned about managing money (or mismanaging it) you learned in childhood.

Creating Jekyll and Hyde

Looking back on the experiences that shaped my ideas about money and my behavior toward it, I now realize I owe much of my money mania (i.e., my Jekyll and Hyde behavior) to my mother. My mother was the first person in my life to teach me valuable money lessons such as how to stretch a dollar, how to balance a checkbook, and the importance of charitable donations and sharing with others. My mother also unwittingly impressed upon me a slew of mixed messages about managing money and budgeting. I grew up somewhat poor in Los Angeles; not dirt poor, but definitely below middle class by any standards. After my parents' divorce when I was around seven years old, my mother was responsible for raising her five daughters alone. She received some financial support from my father, but not enough to make ends meet. As a result, my mother received food stamps and often worked two jobs, holding various positions—cashier, receptionist, secretary—but she never made more than $35,000 in any given year.

Nevertheless, I remember my mother splurging when she wanted to—on us and on herself. When my younger sister, Hope, begged for a Cabbage Patch doll the year these dolls came out, somehow my mother managed to track down those elusive funny-looking dolls—and she came up with the $100 to pay for it. That indulgence likely caused our phone or utilities to get disconnected—sadly a common occurrence during that period. Then there was that one Christmas when my mother bought us an Atari video game system with a complete set of videos. We all loved that. But I'm sure my mother was stressed on January 1 when she didn't have the rent money. And even though we were struggling, my mother made sure we had plenty of food in the house, not to mention the best food available: premium whole-grain bread, top-grade chicken breasts, fresh vegetables, and so forth. When she felt especially generous, my mother indulged her daughters by buying each one of us our own quart of Häagen Dazs ice cream. The cost didn't matter because my mother wanted the best for her girls. As my sister, Deborah, now recalls: "Sure, we had the best food. But I remember what it *really* cost. Having the best meant we ate well for two or three days; then there would be slim pickings for a few days."

Crisis at the Cash Register

When I was about 10 years old in the late 1970s, my mother would routinely send me to a nearby warehouse store called Fedco. It was within walking distance of our apartment complex. My mother would hand me a $20 bill and a list of groceries, saying that it was my responsibility to get everything on the list within budget. Initially, I'd stock up with the first items I came across, but when I'd get to the register and find myself short on cash, I had to put things back. This happened more times than I care to recall. Before long, though, I'd take my mother's list, get everything on it, and come out of Fedco with change to spare. After all, Mom had taught me how to spot deals and how to calculate the cost of items quickly in my head. It's a skill I've never lost. These days whenever I go into Costco, I load up my shopping cart all the while taking a mental inventory and figuring the cost of everything (including tax) in my head. The cashiers at the register are sometimes amazed when I blurt out the total before they even begin to ring up everything; little do they know that I learned "supermarket math" at an early age, mainly to keep from being embarrassed by buying more than I could afford.

My mother also subscribed to the philosophy that since she worked hard, she deserved to be rewarded every now and then. To treat herself, she'd get expensive facials and buy beauty products that she couldn't really afford. After splurging, I would see my mother feverishly writing out her "budget" while sitting at the dining room table. For Mom, a budget mainly was composed of a list of all the many bills she had to pay—bills that invariably exceeded the amount of money she had available. The financial shortfall she faced, along with the stress that resulted from it, were the immediate consequences of her making rash choices with her money. While deciding which debts to pay and which to skip for the month, my mother would often use the phrase that she was, "Robbing Peter to pay Paul." It was the first time I ever heard the expression, and for ill or good it taught me two things: first, when you overspend, you could *choose* whom to pay and when; and second, in order to buy yourself time to pay someone you owe, you could *borrow* money from another source.

Learning What Your Parents Did Not Teach

What messages—overt or subtle—did you pick up from your parents, and what habits did you learn? Many of us can vividly remember our parents, teachers, or other adults teaching us everything from how to tie our shoelaces to how to ride a bike. But what about money? Did anyone ever sit you down and explain to you the basics of how to create a monthly budget? Probably not. Since the goal of this book is to teach you how to become a millionaire, it's important to first walk you through the basics of budgeting and managing cash flow.

> **Your Personal Prosperity Plan is made up of a millionaire budget, a set of written goals, and a financial policy statement.**

I begin with an explanation of the importance of having a budget and then tell you exactly how to create one. For those of you who want to jump-start your budgeting, I give you a simple two-step process for creating a household budget you can live with later in the chapter. I also share practical strategies you can use to avoid blowing your budget. Throughout this chapter you'll learn the three elements that comprise a Personal Prosperity Plan: a millionaire budget, a set of written goals, and a financial policy statement.

Budget Is *Not* A Four-Letter Word

Let's face it. Most people hate being on a budget. Most people, that is, except millionaires. Millionaires not only create personal budgets, but they also stick to them religiously. To millionaires, the budget is a short-term spending plan. It's a detailed outline of what they choose to spend their money on—whether it's their children, travel, home improvements, photography lessons, or some other hobby they enjoy. To a thriving millionaire, developing a well-honed budget is akin to creating a road map for maintaining a comfortable monthly cash flow, meeting financial goals, and measuring financial progress. Millionaires understand the importance of having a budget because they look at it as the foundation for attaining the lifestyle they desire —and for preserving that lifestyle. Budgets have the power to shield you from unforeseen financial calamities, provide a blueprint for managing income and expenses, and even protect you from what is often the biggest obstacle to achieving millionaire status: *you.* Unfortunately, a lot of us can be our own worst enemies; we spend recklessly, charge too much on credit cards, or just flat out mismanage our money. A budget helps keep that in check.

So before you can become a millionaire, it's crucial that you change your mindset about what it means to live on a budget. A budget is part of your Personal Prosperity Plan. However, most of us view a budget as drudgery. We think it's hard to create a budget and even harder to stick to it. We think it's "no fun" living on a budget. Why? Because nine out of ten people believe that the word "budget" is synonymous with the word "can't." As in, "On a budget, I can't have what I really want." Unfortunately, people without a proper view of a budget think living within one really means doing without. We look at living on a budget as deprivation, just as the dieter views the word "diet" as symbolizing all the things that can't be eaten. Well, I don't know about fighting fat, but in the battle to control your finances this notion of deprivation is wrong.

> **A well-honed budget is your road map for maintaining a comfortable monthly cash flow, meeting financial goals, and measuring financial progress.**

In reality, maintaining a budget means that you are actively controlling your money instead of passively allowing your money to control you. It does not mean that you're doing without. On the contrary, people who follow a budget are making choices about what they will do with their money, and in the process deciding what things they will do without for the time being. There's a big difference between doing without because you *have* to, and choosing to do without because you *want* to. In the book *The Overload Syndrome*, author Richard Swenson notes that people with debt problems frequently have to simplify or downsize their lifestyles. Interestingly, he states that 86 percent of the people who simplified their lifestyle by choosing to do without things they really didn't need ended up being happier. This contradicts the bill of goods we're constantly sold by marketers who want us to believe that material things give us happiness. It's a powerful myth and one that most of us fall victim to at one time or another in our lives.

Millionaires have managed, by and large, to escape the lure of Madison Avenue. They don't subscribe to the notion that you have to live large or own the biggest house on the block to prove that you've arrived. Another area in which millionaires part company with the rest of the world is that they do not become stressed over their finances and investments, while most other people do. In fact, by every measure possible, consumers are experiencing unprecedented levels of financial *insecurity*. Consider the following:

- In 2005, a record 2 million households in America filed for bankruptcy protection.

- 65 percent of all U.S. households don't use a basic budget from which to operate each month.

- The average U.S. household carrying a balance on credit cards owes nearly $10,000.

Because of the unprecedented amount of debt consumers are carrying, there's more opportunity than ever to get into financial trouble and mismanage one's finances. And these missteps are now more costly than ever. Even one-time mistakes can have a long-term impact that can damage your credit health for years and jeopardize your overall financial well-being. It's no wonder then that according to an Associated Press poll, seven out of ten Americans feel like their finances are out of control.

Remember how I said millionaires use their budget as a guide to help them figure out what they choose to spend their money on? The benefit of constructing such a budget is that it also helps you determine what *not* to spend (or waste) money on. I like this idea because it helps you put spending in its proper perspective.

Why Most Budgets Don't Work

Budgets alone won't turn you into a millionaire. Yes, it's vital to know what items in your budget are fixed as opposed to which can vary monthly. And, yes, it's important to evaluate those items you're spending money on that are luxuries versus those that are necessities. So why do I say that traditional budget-making recommendations don't work to create millionaires? It's because they're full of restrictions that most people find depressing—or, at the very least, uninspiring. That's a major reason why budgets don't work. People don't stick to them because they're not motivated to stick to them. Another reason many individuals have a tough time living with their budget is that they've created a budget that is completely wrong for them.

A better strategy is to create such an appealing budget that you won't want to sway from it. A millionaire's budget is empowering. It doesn't put you on a fiscal diet. On the contrary,

> **Spend money on the things you want to spend on—just don't spend more than you earn.**

you get to spend your money any way you choose. Love to shop and look like a million bucks? No problem. You can include a shopping allowance in your budget—or anything else you choose—so long as your overall spending decisions adhere to two rules:

1. You cannot spend more than you actually earn.

2. You *should* spend money on the things you *want* to spend it on—not just on things you *have* to pay for.

Sound good so far? OK, stay with me. It gets better. You know why millionaires seem to have it so good? It's because most of them actually enjoy their money and what it can do for them. So here's my suggestion: start practicing the smart habits of millionaires today by means creating a Millionaire-in-Training Budget that is of your own choosing, gives you control over your finances, and contains things that you enjoy spending money on. You will do this by making sure your millionaire's budget is composed of three parts:

1. Necessities.

2. Things that are truly important to you.

3. Things that give you real joy. Let's look closer at each of these areas.

Creating A Millionaire's Budget

You can probably rattle off what your basic necessities are—expenses like housing payments, food, transportation costs, and so on. You may need to think a little longer, however, about the things that are important to you. If education is important to you, you might set aside a portion of your money each month or each year toward educational pursuits—perhaps yours or a family member's. Let's consider also the things that give you joy. In your budget, these should be things that are long-lasting and memorable. A lot of the time experiences and events give us far more joy than material goods and products. Remember that fun family vacation or that romantic getaway you took with your sweetheart? Even when material things are the source of joy, that feeling can often be short-lived, waning even before you've paid the credit card bill for the purchase.

Your Millionaire-in-Training Budget should include categories that give you joy—whether it's travel, philanthropy, a leisure activity, a hobby, or personal care treatments. The idea is to list some things in your budget that you actually *want* to spend money on, as opposed to having only things in your budget on which you *must* spend money.

In my budget, for example, two of the items I include that give me joy are vacations and books. I include these because I love to travel, and I'm a book junkie. But when I take a summer vacation, I don't wait until July rolls around and whip out a credit card to pay for the trip. That's not planning ahead. Instead, I put aside some savings each month to total the amount of money that will be required for that trip. So, if I know I want to spend $1,000 on a trip that starts July 1st, I begin saving for that trip in January, giving me six full months to build up my vacation fund. This way, my spending is well thought out, and I enjoy myself more while I'm on vacation because I don't have to fret about a big credit card bill when I get home.

Some of you may be saying, "In my budget, after I handle my basic necessities, I don't have enough left over to pay for things that give me joy or are important to me." For the present time, don't worry about money that is or is not available. Leave those thoughts alone for now. We'll deal with that shortly. For now, here's what I want you to do. Go grab a piece of paper, a notepad or notebook. (Later, you can put this on a computer spreadsheet if you like. But for the present time, just write it down on paper.) Now list your sources of income by category; next to each source, indicate how much net income (i.e., after taxes) you receive monthly from that source. If you are married, include your spouse's income. Your page should look something like this:

SOURCE OF FUNDS	MONTHLY AMOUNT
salary/wages	$4,300
Commissions	$500
Bonuses	$250
Total net income	$5,050

Some other sources of funds might include:

- Tips
- Part-time income
- Self-employment income
- Interest income

- Dividends
- Alimony
- Social Security
- Pension

Of course, if you have other income, you should add to this list whatever else is relevant and applicable for your situation. Now turn the page over and write these three categories of expenses across the top of the page:

Necessities	Things That Give Me Joy	Important Things

Now list the things that you regularly spend money on in each of these categories. Also write down those things you *wish* you could spend money on. Write out your purchases in the appropriate column. Under "Necessities," you will enter things such as: electric bill, food, or mortgage. Under "Things That Give Me Joy," you might put such items as: gardening supplies or movies/entertainment. Underneath the heading "Important Things," you might include such entries as: college savings or retirement fund. You should have some entries in each category. Take some time to think about what fits into each category—then write everything right down. Don't just keep reading: go get that paper and get to writing. I promise you this exercise will be well worth your time. Please do not skip this part thinking that you'll do it later. Remember what I said earlier about procrastination and lack of discipline being self-imposed obstacles to becoming a millionaire?

Don't Just Dream; Execute By Setting Goals

Too many people dream of becoming a millionaire but have no real plan for how to achieve it. Well, you can't become a millionaire just by dreaming, wanting, or wishing for wealth. As you develop the framework for your millionaire's budget, think about planning for the future and reaching some of your bigger goals. So many times we get caught up in daily tasks and activities that we forget about setting substantive goals for the future. But in order to accrue substantial wealth, it's essential that you write out your short-, medium-, and long-range goals. Some of you may not have thought about your own goals much lately. Perhaps your life has been consumed by your children's world; their needs and wants always come first, and you constantly put your desires on the back burner. It's a mistake to do that. Financially speaking, you can get yourself so wrapped up in another person—whether that individual is your child, partner, or parent—that you neglect yourself and fail to engage in smart, practical financial planning. You don't want to look up 20 years from now and think that you should have managed your money better when you were younger.

To immediately improve how you handle your finances and make a giant leap toward becoming a millionaire, one of the most important things you can do is to write out your personal goals. This one act alone will help you build a foundation for a lifetime of wealth. If you are married or in a committed relationship, I suggest you do this exercise with your partner. Write your individual goals first, and then share your goals with the other person. Ultimately, we are all individuals with our own unique dreams and ambitions. Yet, for those of us involved with significant others, it's crucial that you make a habit of setting—and reaching—your goals together.

I want you to think of your goals in the context of how long it will be before these goals can be realized. Short-term goals should be something that you can accomplish in a relatively brief period of time, say in one to two years, at most. Medium-term goals can be classified as those that require two to ten years to accomplish. Long-range goals are those that require ten years or more to fulfill. To jump start your thinking, I've included a laundry list of goals below. Some of these may be relevant to you; others may hold no significance. The idea, however, is to give yourself permission to focus on the things you want to accomplish in the future—goals you may never have acknowledged to yourself, let alone written down or verbalized to someone else.

> One of the most important things you can do to reach your goal of becoming a millionaire is to write out your personal goals.

Among the goals you might pursue are:

- Eliminating credit card debt.
- Buying a new home.

- Saving for a college education.
- Investing for retirement.
- Starting a business.
- Establishing a cash cushion.
- Paying for a wedding.
- Saving for a new baby.
- Purchasing a vacation home.
- Traveling around the world.
- Buying a boat.
- Paying off student loans.
- Making a large contribution to church, synagogue, etc.
- Buying a new car or a second car.

The Write Way

No matter what your goals, you should know that writing out your plans gives you a far better shot at making them happen. In fact, written goal-setting is a phenomenally powerful act as demonstrated by a number of high-profile cases.

A compelling example of the power of written goal-setting is represented in a 1979 survey of Harvard University students which found that 84 percent of them did not set goals. Another 13 percent of them did set goals, but didn't bother to write them down. And only 3 percent of the graduating class had written goals and an action plan. Ten years later, researchers resurveyed the group. The 13 percent with unwritten goals were earning double the income of those with no goals. But here's the whopper: the 3 percent of the student population with written goals earned 10 times as much as the other 97 percent!

Clearly, written goals are important. But do you realize how it is that written goals are able to propel you to reach success? Here are a few reasons why goal-setting works:

- **PURPOSE:** Goals give your daily and long-term actions meaning and purpose. This helps you stay motivated when you realize that you're engaging in certain financial behaviors for a reason and not just randomly acting.

- **ACCOUNTABILITY:** Goals also make you accountable. If you find that you're regularly falling short of your goals, it could be that you're not really committed to them.

- **STRUCTURE:** Goals provide a framework or structure from which you can operate and achieve your objectives. Many of us need this structure to plug away at reaching our goals, especially long-range visions.

> Written goals give you purpose, make you accountable, make your financial plan concrete, supply you with a discipline to follow, and identify specific areas to focus on.

- **DISCIPLINE:** Goals spur you along to be consistent and disciplined in your actions since you know that a lack of discipline on your part will cause you to deviate from your plans, thereby jeopardizing your chances of hitting your goals.

- **SPECIFICITY:** Goal-setting forces you to not just think about what you want in general terms, but to write down your aims in concrete terms. Adding the element of specificity to your goals makes you far more effective in taking the practical steps required to reach your objectives.

Setting *Smart* Goals

Your goals have to matter to you. They have to be achievable. You want to push yourself and stretch to achieve a goal without putting it so far out of reach that you become disillusioned and give up. Remember, failure is not an option for a Millionaire-in-Training. And I believe that's what you are if you're reading this book and taking this advice seriously. I'm also a believer in setting the appropriate type of goals. SMART is an acronym that describes goals that are:

Specific
Measurable
Action-oriented
Realistic
Time-bound

- *Specific* goals are the exact opposite of vague, hazy dreams. With the latter, someone might say, "I want to be rich," or, "I want to save money for my kid's college education." Those are just general wishes, and chances are they won't be fulfilled. But the person who sets a specific goal would define (in writing) exactly what "rich" means from his or her point of view, as in "I want to have a net worth of $5 million." A specific goal regarding college savings might be: "I want to save $80,000 for my son's college tuition."

When you make goals *measurable,* you quantify the objective you're seeking. In doing so, you ensure accountability and track your progress. For instance, to know where you're going, you have to know your starting point. So if one of your goals is to have no debt, you need to know how much debt you currently have. If you add up your credit card bills and they total $20,000, then you make your goal measurable by writing down something to the effect that, "Over the next two years, I want to eliminate my $20,000 in debt." In light of this goal, you know that after one year, if you're staying on task, you should be able to measure your progress and find that you've knocked out half of your debt, or $10,000.

- *Action-oriented* goals require you to *do* something, not just *think* about doing something. Not weigh your options. Not analyze a certain situation. Not research possibilities, and so forth. No, in order for the goal to carry weight, you must act upon it. So let's say you initially thought that, "I want to start a business," was a goal. That's far too vague. You have to amend that statement and write something along the lines of: "By the end of the month, I want to create a business plan for my new interior design business." This way, you know you actually have to draw up the business plan. If you look up sample business plans on the Internet or investigate what lenders want in a business plan, that's fine as a prerequisite to what you have to do. But ultimately, it's the actual writing of your business plan that you need to accomplish.

■ *Realistic* goals are neither too ambitious nor too easy to accomplish. If you set the bar so high that it's impossible to reach your goal, you're only setting yourself up for failure and disappointment. By all means, make your goals challenging to reach, but be realistic in your expectations. Here's a case in point. Let's say one of your goals is to return to college and obtain an MBA. You already have a Bachelor of Arts degree, and you know that the MBA program you want to attend typically takes two years for the average full-time student to complete. If you work 40 hours a week, will take courses only part time, and can study only on the weekends, don't expect to finish the MBA program in 18 months. Given the confines of your situation, a more realistic yet still challenging goal might be: "I want to earn my MBA in two and a half years."

Any worthwhile goal is *time-bound* and includes a deadline by which the goal should be met. When you include a deadline, you make your goal time-bound. Therefore, it's not good enough to say: "I plan to buy a new home." Instead, when writing out your SMART goal, put down something like: "Two years from now, I plan to put down a 10 percent down payment toward the purchase a $450,000 Tudor home with four bedrooms and two bathrooms." This goal is clearly specific, measurable, action-oriented, realistic for many people, and time-bound.

DOES THE COUPLE THAT SETS GOALS TOGETHER STAY TOGETHER?

Again, after you write out your goals, I urge you to share them with your spouse, or significant other, and have the spouse or significant other show you his or her goals. You may be surprised to see what some of your partner's goals are. It's helpful to do this because then you both have an idea about where each person wants to spend money. You can also see where you have goals in common. Being aligned with each other, in terms of long-term goals, can be an especially strong way to bond with your partner. That's no small task given the amount of financial fighting that goes on with most couples. Did you know that, among couples who divorce, financial strife is one of the biggest reasons for the break up? Seventy percent of all divorced people cite money squabbles as a reason, at least in part, for their divorce. If you see a goal that your partner would like to accomplish in the future, now is the time to begin talking about how the two of you will meet that goal. So let's say you want to go back to school in a year, and he wants to launch a new business in a year. How do you prioritize your goals? Compromises will often have to be made, but at least you've began the process of bringing your dreams to fruition—by putting those goals on paper and considering what steps are required to get you to them.

PUTTING A PRICE TAG ON YOUR GOALS

Part of getting there also means figuring out how much your goals will cost. You likely already know the cost associated with reaching many short- or medium-term goals, like eliminating that $7,000 in credit card debt you have, or purchasing that new $1,500 computer you've been eyeing. So go ahead and write down their costs next to the goals you've already listed. However, there may be some goals, especially those that are long term, that you honestly have no idea of their true expense. Do you know what college will cost 15 years from now? Or do you have any idea how much retirement will cost three decades from now? Fortunately, there are tools you can use to help you figure out the costs of those far-away goals. The single best tool is at your fingertips on the Internet. Just be selective about the sites and tools you use. There is a dizzying array of options to choose from; select sites and tools that are accredited.

Now that you've written out some SMART goals and figured out how much they will cost, we can return to our discussion about your Millionaire-in-Training Budget.

The Four Problems with Most Budgets

In the course of coaching people nationwide about their finances, I've found that most individuals who have difficulty living on a monthly budget suffer from one of four problems:

1. They've never truly itemized their expenses; consequently, their spending exceeds their income.
2. They exclude two key categories from their budget: savings and goals.
3. They've created a budget that is excessively frugal.
4. They blow their budgets because of poor planning.

Let's address each of these problems and explain how you will rectify them to create a more satisfying, wealth-building Millionaire-in-Training Budget.

MILLIONAIRES DON'T GUESS ABOUT MONEY

For those of you who have never actually itemized your monthly expenses, you're really operating without a budget, although you may think that you do have a budget since you know roughly what you're spending. But the reality is that rough numbers and guesstimates won't do—and they certainly have no place in the millionaire's budget. To create a Millionaire-in-Training Budget you need to know your exact expenditures: how much you spend on utilities, what your transportation costs are, your monthly food bill, and so forth. This is the only way you'll be able to ascertain how much slack is in your budget for things beyond "necessities." Having full knowledge about your expenses also aids you in making adjustments to your budget when necessary—especially during times when money is tight.

PREPARING FOR THE DREADED Ds

When you create your budget, don't overlook two important categories. The Millionaire-in-Training Budget always includes money that is to be set aside for two crucial things: savings and goals. It's vital that you put away money for savings because these funds will act as your safety net when something goes wrong. And trust me: something will always go wrong that will cost you money. It might be a car accident, a leaky roof, or a relative in dire need of a loan. But the day will come when you will have to spend money that you didn't anticipate. Many of you know what I'm talking about because it seems like every other month or every other week some unexpected expense pops up. Some things are relatively minor. But then there is what I call the six Dreaded Ds: downsizing, divorce, disability, disease or death in the family, and disaster. If you're not careful, any of these occurrences can put a crimp in your finances and throw your budget out of whack. But when you have a savings cushion, you can weather these financial crises large and small. Your savings account will have to be built up over time. I recommend that you have three months' worth of expenses set aside. So if your monthly bills are $3,000, then you should have a savings cushion of $9,000 on hand. So here's what you need to do. Go back to your budget and, if you don't already have savings listed, add it under the category marked "Necessities."

FINDING HIDDEN MONEY IN YOUR BUDGET

You also need to save for the goals you've written down. You should have already assigned a cost to your goals. Some of these aims, like your own retirement in 20 years, will have very hefty price tags. Now here's the part where you're probably wondering: How can I save for long-range goals, things I enjoy, or things that make me happy when it's tough to just stay on top of my current bills and necessities? Well, the answer is: you have to prioritize how you spend your money, and you must also be willing to make small commitments to your goals now so that they will actually be reached. Here's how you can prioritize to add both savings and money for goals into your budget. Cut back on so-called necessities that are really luxuries. That's where you'll find some hidden money in your budget. I often cite cable television as a case in point. There are people out there who will tell me that the $89.99 a month they pay for premium cable service, complete with 200 channels, is a necessity. Come on! That's a luxury. You don't *need* to have premium cable. For all you avid television watchers: if you can't stomach the idea of deleting cable entirely from your budget, at least consider ratcheting your premium cable package down to a more affordable basic cable service.

Check out your budget and look for other areas where you've really classified your wants as your needs. You might have 15 short-, medium-, and long-range goals listed. If your budget is especially tight, I don't expect you to put aside money for all 15 things at once.

Do what's realistic. Instead of adding all 15 goals to your budget at once, you might add three, starting a fund this month to save for the one short-term goal, one medium-range goal, and one long-term goal. The idea is to get started saving now, rather than procrastinating. If you put off saving, you'll never get around to stashing the money away, thereby putting those goals further and further out of your reach. Even if you can put aside only $10 a month, start doing so immediately. Over time, as your cash flow improves and you begin to build wealth, you'll be able to add more money to that goal, and begin saving for other goals as well.

ARE MILLIONAIRES CHEAPSKATES?

Believe it or not, a millionaire budget is not a cheapskate budget. The third mistake most people make when creating a budget is that they make it far too restrictive. Why make a budget that you hate, that is impossible to live with, and that forces to you live like a complete miser? In order to have a Millionaire-in-Training Budget, you have to be willing to stick to it, and the best way to do this is to give yourself room to spend on things that are important to you. You need to love your budget so that you're motivated to work within the parameters you've created. It's pointless to set up a budget so tight that you have no wiggle room for the occasional unanticipated purchase, no flexibility to increase or decrease your spending in certain categories, and absolutely no room for error. That's like going on a diet to lose 20 pounds and telling yourself that you won't eat any sweets or carbohydrates—for the rest of your natural life. How realistic is that?

THE PITFALLS OF POOR PLANNING

The fourth mistake that many people make is that they consistently spend more than their budgets allow. To avoid this pitfall, remember that unexpected events and emergencies will always come up. That's life. But you can minimize the impact of these occurrences—and turn your ordinary budget into a full-fledged Millionaire-in-Training Budget—by adjusting your budget according to the principle of LIFE. LIFE is an acronym that describes the four ways that your budget gets out of whack forcing you to spend more than you planned for the month, or causing you to live from paycheck to paycheck.

In **LIFE**:

L —Listed items are undercalculated.

I —Impulse purchases seduce you.

F —Forgotten bills surface.

E —Emergencies or unexpected events occur.

Once you realize that LIFE happens to everyone, you can take some steps to safeguard your finances and create a realistic budget you can live with. And for most of us, that's the first step in having fewer money problems and achieving financial freedom.

The Millionaire-In-Training Budget Made Easy

There's a simple, two-step system you can use to create your very own powerful and practical Millionaire-in-Training Budget, one that will help you achieve peace of mind and eliminate worries about your money.

STEP 1: MAKE A LIST OF YOUR INCOME AND EXPENSES.

Itemize your income and all the different areas of your life in which you spend money. (By the way, you should have done this by now.) Some common categories are:

- Food
- Housing
- Entertainment

- Transportation
- Debts
- Utilities
- Educational costs
- Child care
- Insurance
- Miscellaneous

When you make your expenses list, take a moment to think about how you really live your life on a daily and monthly basis. Do you have kids for whom you regularly buy gifts? If so, include a gifts category for things like birthdays, holidays, graduations, or other special occasions. Or maybe you're an avid reader. If that's the case, enter a category for monthly magazine subscriptions or books you purchase. Remember, by including in your budget things that you enjoy and things that are important to you, you won't feel deprived, and ultimately you'll be more likely to stick to your budget.

STEP 2: ADJUST TO AVOID BUDGET-BUSTERS.

If your expenses exceed your income, you'll have to cut back in areas that aren't necessities.

Again, think about the acronym LIFE. Use the principles I explain about LIFE to see where you need to tweak your budget. And don't forget that your Millionaire-in-Training Budget absolutely *must* include money set aside for emergency savings and for goals. Otherwise, anytime a financial calamity strikes, you won't have cash on hand to deal with the crisis, and you'll have to resort to using credit and going into debt. Without a cash cushion, you'll only tread water. You'll constantly feel like no matter what you do with your finances, you're always taking one step forward and two steps back. Additionally, if you don't allocate any money for your goals, needless to say, they'll never be reached.

Remember that having a good budget offers a host of benefits. A well-made budget:

- Gives you power and control over your finances.
- Keeps you from living paycheck to paycheck.
- Allows you to save for future goals and dreams.
- Helps you avoid going into debt.

And to top it off, a well-prepared budget is one of the basic financial tools that will set you on the path to becoming a millionaire. Get your Millionaire-in-Training Budget together today. Come on, you can do it! Even if you are battling a split personality, the "good" part of you can conquer the "bad" part. When you get your budget done, you're on the road to becoming a millionaire. Isn't that worth it?

Copy the Habits of the Rich

Now that you've created your Millionaire-in-Training Budget, your next task is to make a Financial Policy Statement. I know that many of you have probably never heard of such a document. This is similar to an investment policy statement that is used by high net worth individuals and institutional investors. This statement helps them establish criteria for buying or selling stocks and bonds. In its most basic terms, the investment policy statement is a black-and-white reminder about why people are investing and under what circumstances they should drop an investment. By defining their investment criteria up front, these sophisticated investors take the emotion out of investing when new opportunities arise or when conditions change for investments they own. You'll learn more about how to become a successful investor in Chapter 5.

For now, let's consider your Financial Policy Statement. It is a written document that contains a broad set of financial rules that you make and live by when handling, spending, and managing personal finances.

The document should reflect your personal values and goals, and it should reference the things that are important to you. When you create a Financial Policy Statement—and it can be as short as a few sentences or so—what you're doing, to a certain extent, is defining the parameters by which you will control your money, and control yourself.

CREATING YOUR OWN FINANCIAL POLICY STATEMENT

Let's suppose that you create a Financial Policy Statement that is based on the following assumptions: you are 38 years old, married with two school-age children, and you and your spouse, who is 40, have agreed on the following long-, medium-, and short-term goals:

1. Begin saving much more aggressively for retirement by ages 55 and 57, respectively.
2. Trade up to a new, bigger home within five years.
3. Knock out your $3,500 in credit card debt in less than a year.

Given this scenario, here is a sample Financial Policy Statement:

> It's crucial that we become debt-free and remain that way. We realize that in order to stay out of debt, we must not overspend. It is also important to us to retire early in order to devote more time to our family. We believe that certain short-term sacrifices are worth making in order to achieve longer-term objectives. In our household, we desire to work together cooperatively to support each other and achieve our personal, professional, and financial goals. We will spend our money wisely on the things that we enjoy, such as travel, and will make joint decisions on big-ticket purchases. We will strive to be good, responsible financial role models for our children, providing them with the education, safety, love, and the financial security they deserve.

As you can see, this Financial Policy Statement covers a lot of ground. It's not too specific and doesn't dictate your exact day-to-day activities. But it does offer overarching principles that will govern your daily life. A Financial Policy Statement is not written in stone, though. It should be viewed as a living, breathing document, something that changes as your life, personal needs, goals, and circumstances change.

When creating your Financial Policy Statement, use phrases like: "It's important to me/us that..." or, "I/We believe that..." or, "In my/our household..." to guide your thinking. Make the document as short or long as you like. Personalize your Financial Policy Statement, and make your declarations authentic and realistic for you. Review the document regularly—as often as you can stand it, in fact. I recommend you look at it at least weekly. It will remind you in broad terms of how you should be running your financial affairs. As you start to memorize parts of your Financial Policy Statement and internalize the ideas it expresses, you'll probably find that your actions don't always follow the letter and spirit of your intentions, as outlined in your statement. For instance, maybe you've done something foolish in handling your money, and upon reflection you realize that you haven't been setting a good example for your children. Don't beat yourself up over that. The important thing is to maintain and follow your Financial Policy Statement as diligently as possible—the longer you keep to the rules outlined in the statement, the quicker you'll be able to practice these policies on autopilot.

Other ideas that could be incorporated into a Financial Policy Statement are:

- I will avoid making impulse purchases.
- We want to achieve balance in our spending, neither overindulging nor depriving ourselves.
- It's important to me to arrange my financial affairs so that I am not a burden to anyone.

- In my household, I strive to save 15 percent of my earnings.
- I believe that a portion of my money should be used to help others.

Hopefully, you've got the hang of this and can modify these phrases, or generate entirely different, unique statements as your situation changes. I hope you can also see that the three parts of your Personal Prosperity Plan—setting written goals, creating a Millionaire-in-Training Budget, and defining your Financial Policy Statement—all work together. After all, your monthly spending activities should be related to your future goals and values about how your overall finances are managed.

No Plan—But You Can Always Play the Lottery, Right? Wrong!

If you don't create a Personal Prosperity Plan, one alternative path to becoming a millionaire is to "get lucky" and win the lottery, right? I'm downright shocked at how many people—well-intentioned but sadly misguided—play the lottery on a regular basis under the false belief that "instant" riches are their only way out of financial misery. In a December 4, 2005 front-page article by Judy DeHaven and Robert Gebeloff about the New Jersey state lottery, the *Star Ledger* featured a woman named Pat Howard. Howard, an insurance agent from Newark, New Jersey, is known locally as the "Queen of the Lottery." By her own estimates, Howard spends between $20 and $30 *every day* on lottery tickets, the *Star Ledger* said. Translation: she's doling out $600 to $900 a month, or $7,200 to $10,800 each year, for the remote opportunity of striking it rich. Too bad she doesn't realize that she could be putting all that money to much better use.

You've got as much chance of winning a huge lottery as you do of finding a needle in the proverbial haystack. But let's say, for the sake of argument, that you actually do hit it big and win a lottery jackpot. Do you think your financial problems would end? I hate to be the bearer of bad news, but, unfortunately, for most individuals, winning the lottery would actually be the start of a whole new set of woes. Take a look below at this fascinating list of people who got "lucky" winning various lotteries. And then see what happened to them after their "good fortune."

WINNING A LOTTO (MIS)FORTUNE

According to an article entitled "Unlucky Lottery Winners Who Lost Their Money" by Ellen Goodstein from Bankrate.com, which reported the following information, lottery winners frequently are dogged by their own poor money management, greedy relatives, and other schemers out to get their piece of the pie. As Bankrate.com noted, here are instances in which lottery winners thought they had achieved the American dream, but wound up living a nightmare:

> Evelyn Adams of New Jersey won the lottery in the Garden State not once, but twice—first in 1985 and again in 1986. All told, she received $5.4 million. Today, Adams lives in a trailer, and the money is completely gone. What happened? Adams admits she had a gambling addiction. Plus, practically everyone she knew wanted a handout. "Winning the lottery isn't always what it's cracked up to be," Adams told Bankrate.com.

> William "Bud" Post of Pennsylvania won $16.2 million in that state's lottery in 1988. Within a year, he was $1 million in debt and later declared bankruptcy. He later lived on food stamps and Social Security of $450 a month. What happened? An ex-girlfriend sued him for a share of his winnings. His own brother, who hoped to inherit some of the lottery money, was arrested for hiring a hit man to kill Post. And other siblings

convinced Post to invest in unprofitable businesses that caused more family squabbles. "I wish it never happened. It was totally a nightmare," Post said of his lottery experience, adding: "I'm tired, I'm over 65 years old, and I just had a serious operation for a heart aneurysm. Lotteries don't mean (anything) to me," he said in 2004. Mr. Post died in January 2006, Bankrate.com reported in March 2006.

Suzanne Mullins of Virginia won $4.2 million in the Virginia lottery in 1993. Today, she's flat broke and deep in debt. What happened? She borrowed $197,746.15 from a company and agreed to pay back the loan with her yearly checks from the Virginia lottery through 2006. The state lottery changed the rules, though, permitting Mullins to collect her winnings in a lump sum. So she went ahead and cashed in the remaining amount—but failed to make her loan payments. Mullins said the unpaid debt was largely due to a lengthy illness suffered by her uninsured son-in-law, who needed $1 million to cover his medical bills. Mark Kidd, the attorney representing the company that sued Mullins for nonpayment, said the company won a judgment for $154,147, but hasn't collected a dime. "My understanding is she has no assets," the lawyer said.

Ken Proxmire of Michigan won $1 million in his state lottery. Within five years, he went bankrupt. Today he has a regular job and keeps a low profile. What happened? He relocated to California and joined his brothers in the car business. But it didn't work out. Proxmire also gave too much to others. His son, Rick, told Bankrate.com: "It was a hell of a good ride for three or four years, but now he lives more simply. There's no more talk of owning a helicopter or riding in limos. We're just everyday folk. Dad's now back to work as a machinist."

MORE MONEY, MORE PROBLEMS

Lest you think these examples from Bankrate.com are complete aberrations, let me add to this list stories of three other individuals involved in more recent, well-publicized cases of lottery winnings. Sadly, their lives also went awry after hitting big jackpots.

Mack Metcalf and Virginia Merida of Kentucky, the estranged married couple, shared a $34 million lottery jackpot in 2000. By 2001, they were divorced. Today, both are dead. In 2003, Metcalf died at age 45 from complications related to alcoholism, according to a report in the *New York Times*. In 2005, on the day before Thanksgiving, Merida's partially decomposed body was found in her home. Authorities were looking into whether the 51-year-old Merida was the victim of a drug overdose, the *Times* noted. What happened? Reports say that substance abuse plagued the couple, along with lawsuits, family troubles, and lavish spending on expensive homes, vintage cars, and other luxuries.

Jack Whittaker of West Virginia holds the record for the largest single prize ever awarded by a lottery, a $314.9 million Powerball jackpot won on Christmas Day, 2002. Whittaker was 55 when he bought his winning ticket. He opted for the one-time payout, netting a lump sum of $113 million after taxes. Unfortunately, since scoring that big prize, Whittaker has encountered a dizzying array of problems—from getting robbed multiple times to being arrested twice for drunk driving to enduring the drug-related death of the 17-year-old granddaughter he showered with money and gifts. Today, Whittaker faces a morass of legal woes, the fallout from millions of squandered dollars, and stressed family relationships. What happened? One year after his win, Whittaker told the Associated Press that he'd already spent $45 million, much of it on property. But other things also took a huge financial and personal toll. Beggars—many of them complete strangers to Whittaker—came out of the woodwork. Whittaker also dropped tons of money at casinos and strip clubs, according to published reports. And his wife of nearly 40 years, who previously adored him, is now divorcing Whittaker. Whittaker's estranged wife, Jewel, blames the Powerball jackpot for destroying her family. She told the *Charleston Gazette*: "I wish I would have torn the ticket up." In a December 2005 interview with a local FOX-TV reporter, Mrs. Whittaker said that in 2006 she will start writing a book that shares the message that money can't buy happiness.

The Reality about Sudden Wealth

Now, in light of all the horror tales you have just read, I ask: Do you still think that coming into sudden money via the lottery is the dream of a lifetime? Clearly it is not. Having instant millions is actually dangerous and disastrous if you have no concept of how to properly manage money. And regrettably, the vast majority of people out there are poor money managers. Sudden wealth will also only exacerbate personal shortcomings or vices you now have—such as compulsive spending or excessive drinking. Additionally, big windfalls tend to intensify conflicts among relatives or bring to the surface hot-button issues that may have been simmering for years. You think there's drama right now in your family? Toss a few million dollars into the picture, and watch how explosive things can truly become. So, sure, it would be great to enjoy a monetary windfall—*if* you have proper money-management skills; *if* you have correct financial guidance from experts who have your best interests at heart; and *if* you are emotionally prepared for the impact of such a change in your life. But those are three monumental ifs. And unfortunately, most individuals are sorely lacking in all these areas. So the next time you think, "If only I could become a millionaire by winning the lottery," be careful what you wish for. Those lottery winnings can be fleeting—and cause grief you never expected. By the way, the same thing applies to any other kind of windfall, whether it's an inheritance from a dead relative, a payout from an insurance policy, or proceeds from a lawsuit settlement.

> **Having instant millions is actually dangerous and disastrous if you have no concept of how to properly manage money.**

It's far better to become a millionaire through your own merit and solid planning—not because of luck. Stick to the Millionaire Success Formula that I'm teaching you, and you'll have your own fortune soon enough, along with the skills, expert assistance, and the proper mindset to handle that money. Your seven-step plan to becoming a millionaire begins with the foundation you've just laid. You have just created your Personal Prosperity Plan: a millionaire budget, a set of written goals, and a Financial Policy Statement represent your ticket to long-lasting riches, not some randomly-selected, computer-generated lottery game card.

2

INVEST FIRST, LAST, AND ALWAYS IN YOUR REPUTATION

If you've read other books on wealth-building, you already know that, when it comes to investing, nearly all personal finance experts focus on telling you how to buy and sell stocks, bonds, real estate, or other assets. As your Money Coach I want to tell you something revolutionary in terms of managing your personal finances and becoming a millionaire. It goes against conventional wisdom, and it's a secret of which most people are totally oblivious. The single best thing you can do to become wealthy is to invest in yourself by investing in your *reputation*. This means that you're far more likely to build wealth by being the best you can be and betting on yourself, rather than by placing money on any stock reported on Wall Street.

Investing in yourself will help you reap millions of dollars over a lifetime, and it will also help you experience an abundantly satisfying personal and professional life. Throughout this chapter, I reveal how investing in yourself leads to more of everything including income, savings, respect, status, favors from others, and even happiness. You can generate millions in cash and rack up an impressive array of non-financial returns by investing in yourself, making you the ultimate blue-chip investment. What's more is that you are making a lifetime stake in yourself, without the risk of fluctuating markets that affect the stock market.

Investing in yourself will help you reap millions of dollars over a lifetime.

There are six primary ways you can invest in yourself and enhance your reputation. It's SIMPLE:

S — Strive for perfect credit.

I — Improve your education.

M— Make it a lifelong endeavor to increase your knowledge, training, and skills.

P — Put money in your own business before anyone else's.

L — Learn to give back.

E — Earn more by creating stability in your personal and professional life.

I used a number of acronyms throughout the book to help you understand and remember a principle or lesson I'm trying to teach. In Chapter 1, I outline the concept of LIFE and used it to describe the four ways life can throw your budget out of whack. In this chapter, I elaborate on the abbreviation SIMPLE to show you how easy it is and why it's so desirable to invest in yourself above and beyond everything else. The word PERFECT is also used as an acronym for my unique seven-step system for achieving perfect credit. It's a system I've never revealed—until now.

What Defines "Perfect" Credit?

In the sometimes harsh world of personal finances, the number one thing that improves your reputation is having outstanding credit. While you can and should devote considerable energy to investing in yourself by using all six methods provided in this chapter, the most powerful strategy you can employ to enhance your financial reputation is to strive for perfect credit. I define perfect credit in two ways: First and foremost, perfect credit is illustrated by a mysterious three-digit number—called a FICO score—that dominates your financial life. FICO scores range from 300 to 850. The higher your score, the better your credit standing. While it's not necessary to have an 850 score to qualify as having perfect credit, your FICO score should be in the top-tier range, which is from 760 to 850. Having perfect credit means that you can use the strength of your good name alone, and sign on the dotted line to get direct access to a whole host of products and services including mortgages, automobiles, credit cards, business lines of credit, and personal loans—at the most favorable terms available in the marketplace. By the way, FICO scores are so-named because FICO is an abbreviation for the Minneapolis-based Fair Isaac & Co., which calculates credit scores for tens of millions of people.

Better Than Money in the Bank

Having outstanding credit should be a goal that you relentlessly pursue. It's not enough to have average or even good credit. To join the ranks of millionaires, having stellar credit is a must. In many instances, having an outstanding credit reputation is often better than having cash in the bank. How so? You can often get access to cash, in the form of loans, grants, and other aid, based solely on the strength of your credit report. And, whereas you may have $100,000 in cold, hard dollars on hand, having perfect credit could give you access to 20 times that amount of money—or more. Before I describe the numerous other benefits having perfect credit brings, let's look at what happens when you have the converse of perfect credit—lousy credit.

Battling a Bad Reputation

Any time a financial institution, credit card company, bank, or other entity puts a negative mark on your credit file, what it's doing is bad-mouthing you to the rest of the world. It's telling anyone who cares to listen that you were 30 days (or more) late in paying a bill, and it's damaging your reputation in the process. After all, when you have late payments or really serious blemishes on your credit report—such as a charge-off, judgment, repossession, or foreclosure—you've essentially been branded as a financial deadbeat. Like many people, you may have gotten into financial trouble through no fault of your own, say in the wake of a job layoff. Or maybe you fell behind on your debts because of extenuating circumstances, such as an illness that resulted in medical bills your insurance company wouldn't cover. Nevertheless, a bad credit history puts a host of people and institutions on notice that you're not to be trusted. Poor credit implies that you can't or won't honor your obligations, that your word is not your bond, and that, from a financial point of view, you're a bad risk. You wind up with the economic equivalent of a scarlet letter simply because you didn't pay some bills on time.

It's very difficult to restore a financial reputation once it's been damaged, where one mistake can hurt your credit for seven years. Blemishes in your credit file can plague your reputation for what feels like an eternity, hampering your ability to increase your net worth and become a millionaire. Having spectacular credit makes life so much easier—and being burdened with lousy credit can be one of the most stressful, frustrating things you'll ever face. I know, because I've experienced both extremes first hand.

Sign on the Dotted Line

At one point in my adult life, I considered renting a town house. When I visited it for the first time, a helpful, friendly manager at the housing complex raved about the property's many amenities, highlighted its prestigious location, and assured me that the school district ranked among the best in the state. After I decided I wanted the place, the good-natured manager suddenly turned all business. She briskly reviewed my written application, asked me for a security deposit, and then told me point blank: "If your credit is good, no problem. You'll get approved. If your credit is bad, you won't." Clearly, she had done this many times before. I smiled, looked her dead in the eyes and replied with confidence: "My credit is perfect. So I'm sure I'll be moving in soon." With that, she immediately went online to get my credit report. In less than three minutes, she examined practically every financial detail about me for the past dozen years: mortgages I had paid off, cars I owned, my credit card balances, and, of course, my payment history for all these things. When she was satisfied that not a single blemish was to be found, she pulled herself away from her computer terminal, swiveled around in her black leather chair, faced me again, and said pleasantly: "You have very excellent credit. When would you like to sign the lease?" It was a done deal.

Red Carpet Treatment

Weeks later, as I began furnishing my new residence, I paid for certain household goods upfront. However, for two big-ticket furniture purchases, I opted to take advantage of zero percent financing deals. In the first store, the sales clerk ran my credit. Then he quickly told me that I qualified for the best terms available. At the second retail establishment, a saleswoman asked me whether I was sure I wanted to apply for credit. "Citi Financial is very strict. You have to have really good credit, or they reject you," she warned me. I suppose she wanted to spare me the embarrassment of being declined if my credit wasn't stellar. I told her to proceed, and two minutes later I was approved. "Is there anything else you'd like to buy," the saleswoman now asked, "because you have a line of credit up to $7,500." In all these instances, I received the proverbial red carpet treatment based entirely on the strength of my credit standing. Here's why: My credit card debt was minimal, I had a 760 FICO score, and my triple-A credit report would make even Donald Trump green with envy. But it wasn't always this way.

The Bad Credit Blues

I used to have terrible credit. Not just bad credit—I'm talking truly awful credit: multiple late payments, charge-offs, court judgments for nonpayments, and even an automobile repossession marred my credit file. While I never had the granddaddy of poor credit—a bankruptcy—I nevertheless had the kind of credit file that must have made bank officers sit around and laugh out loud. I can just picture them reviewing my credit card application. We'll call them Joe and Harold.

> JOE: Hey, Harry, you gotta get a load of this one!!! Can you believe she even applied?! What was she thinking—or should I say, what was she smoking—to even remotely hope she would get approved? Maybe instead of our form rejection letter, we can write her and say: "Due to your pitiful payment history, young lady, you aren't getting a credit card, a loan, or anything else for years to come!" Ha, ha, ha!

Well, OK, so maybe that's a stretch. Perhaps the many credit card rejection letters I received just got spit out by some computer, and no one personally gloated over my sorry state of affairs. But I have to figure that, at my worst, when my credit score was no doubt in the low 500s, I was unquestionably a classic case of "How to Ruin Your Credit in No Time Flat."

Easy Credit, Courtesy of Your College Campus

Like many of you, I got my first credit card as a college freshman. In fact, the day I moved into my on-campus apartment at the University of California at Irvine, I walked into the modest room I would share with my roommate and saw that credit card applications had been placed on the beds. No sheets; no blankets—just "special invitations" courtesy of MasterCard, VISA, and American Express. "Wow! I must really be an adult now," I figured. "I can get a credit card in my own name." I soon discovered that credit card offers were rampant on campus. They were posted in the student center, stapled on message boards, thumb-tacked or taped onto poles, and piled high on tables anywhere students hung out. And, of course, any walls that had those handy brochure holders affixed to them—and there always seemed to be tons of those holders right outside large lecture halls—were sure to be stuffed with credit card solicitations from any number of banks and financial institutions. That was 20 years ago. If you walk the halls of most college campuses today, you'll see that not much has changed.

Financially Illiterate College Student + Too Much Credit = Financial Disaster

Some of the credit card marketing I encountered as a student was subtle. But most of it was in-your-face, no holds barred. "Want a free T-shirt?" asked credit card solicitors as I strolled from one class to another. Sure, why not? I thought. Like most 18-year-old college kids, my mind was somehow automatically programmed to gravitate toward four-letter words like *free*. "Great . . . . just fill out this credit card application," they urged. I went to buy textbooks at the book store—expensive books, I might add. And what happened there? Along with my books and receipts, the cashiers stuffed more credit card offers into my plastic shopping bags.

While all this credit was being thrown at me, nobody told me how to manage it responsibly. Forget the fact that I didn't even have a job. Nobody advised me that, just because I qualified for a $5,000 credit line, didn't mean I should accept it. Nobody cautioned me to make my payments every month without fail—or those late payments would haunt me for seven years. Nobody taught me that making minimum payments on credit cards with 20 percent interest rates basically meant I'd be in debt for life. So I guess it's no surprise—some might say it was inevitable—that by the time I was just 21 years old, I owed nearly $10,000 to a slew of creditors. Making matters worse, the first car I'd ever purchased, a 1987 Hyundai Excel, wound up being hauled off by the repo man—despite my frequent efforts to hide the vehicle blocks away.

The Road to Recovery—Sort of

Luckily, after earning my Bachelor's degree in 1991, I got a job, negotiated fiercely with bill collectors, and started paying off the many debts I'd accumulated in college. From that point on, I became diligent about always paying my bills on time. I never again wanted to deal with irate debt collectors and their annoying phone calls at all hours of the day and night. Even after having learned my lesson about no late payments ever and after earning my Master's degree in 1993, I still wasn't schooled in the proper use of credit and how to manage debt wisely. In fact, as time went on, I used credit more and more—almost as if it was cash. I actually thought I was being a responsible credit user because I was making minimum payments each month without fail. Little did I know that I was fooling myself and allowing myself to be seduced by the lure of easy credit. Unfortunately, "buy now, pay later" became my financial motto.

Debt Free at Last

By the time I was in my early 30s, I was swimming in debt—$100,000 worth of credit card debt to be exact. Fortunately, I managed to pay it all off in less than three years without resorting to bankruptcy. In 2004, when I paid off the last of my massive credit card debt, I finally began to enjoy the benefits of having zero debt and outstanding credit.

Topping the list of benefits is peace of mind. I never have to sweat over my credit card possibly being rejected when paying for a dinner out with friends, paying for a hotel room, or buying any kinds of goods and services. Nor do I fret over whether I'll be approved for anything. Banks fall all over themselves now competing for my business.

The Pleasures of Perfect Credit

I'm guessing that given the chance, you'd also want perfect credit—and the pleasure of a smooth, hassle-free process when you're ready to acquire a gold credit card, finance a new car, or buy a home. When you're applying for a loan and you have perfect credit, it's like playing Monopoly and having a "Get out of Jail Free" card up your sleeve with every roll. But having perfect credit affords you more than just the best rates and terms on loans. It also means that you'll pay far less for life and auto insurance. Moreover, people with outstanding credit get promotions on the job and new job offers far more readily than do people with poor credit histories. Did you know that, under the law, your existing employer, or a prospective employer, can legally check your credit and use that information as the basis for making a promotion or hiring decision about you? Compared to a person with bad credit, the individual with stellar credit saves a remarkable amount of money and earns a lot more too.

The Story of Bill and Skip

Here's a tale about two 40-year-old guys who are best friends; we'll call them Bill and Skip. From the time they were teenagers, both Bill and Skip dreamed of becoming successful corporate sales executives and enjoying the finer things in life. Bill and Skip both attended the same college, and both graduated with business degrees and a 3.5 grade point average. They both married around the same time, and now each has two kids of the same ages, seven and five. Since Bill and Skip are sports buffs, neither one smokes; in fact, the two of them are in great shape because they work out together every weekend at the local gym. Although Bill and Skip both work for the same Fortune 500 company, that's where the similarities end. Bill always pays his bills on time. He's made it a point in his life to handle his financial affairs responsibly. So he keeps his debts at manageable levels, always keeps up with his obligations, and safeguards his credit in every way he can, even making mortgage payments 10 days ahead of the due date.

Skip, on the other hand, plays a lot more fast and loose with his finances. He skips Visa payments every now and then, sometimes just because he's too busy to get stamps from the Post Office. Because he's on the road so much, Skip often forgets to mail his cell phone payment when it's due. "What's the big deal if I pay it a couple days late?" Skip thinks. "They're still going to get their money." Additionally, Skip has missed making his mortgage payment on time twice in the last year—once when he was on vacation and another time when he was traveling for a business conference. The same thing happened with his Lexus payment. Unfortunately, Skip didn't have automatic payments set up online to make those payments in his absence. "I can't be bothered with that. Those things are too complicated, and, besides, I'm too busy," he said when his wife suggested putting their bills on automatic payment plans to avoid those constant late fees. Skip's wife was tired of arguing with him about their money problems, so she just let it go.

But when it came time for Bill and Skip to get loans and insurance, the wayward Skip was shocked at how much he had to pay compared to Bill. When the two friends compared notes, here's what they found:

- **MORTGAGES:** Although Bill and Skip both took out 30-year, fixed-rate mortgages for $400,000, Bill's monthly payment is $2,300, while Skip's is $2,800. Compared to Skip, Bill's mortgage payments are $6,000 less per year, saving Bill $180,000 over the life of his loan.

- **AUTO LOANS:** Both men made equal down payments to finance their late model Lexus automobiles, but Bill's payment is $400 a month, while Skip has to pay $550 monthly. By the time the cars are paid off, in five years, Bill will have doled out $9,000 less than Skip. And, since the average American family buys seven new cars in a lifetime, that $9,000 gets multiplied sevenfold for a total lifetime savings of $63,000 for Bill.

- **CREDIT CARDS:** Bill and Skip are both carrying $3,000 balances on their Visa credit cards. However, since Bill has perfect credit, his interest rate is just 8.9 percent; Skip's is at the default rate of 28.99 percent. So Bill pays around $27 in monthly interest, while Skip is hit with interest charges of $87 each month. In five years' time, Bill saves $3,600 in interest costs. At this rate, over the next 30 years, Bill will pay $108,000 less in finance charges.

- **LIFE INSURANCE:** Both men bought $500,000 whole life insurance policies. But Bill's cost him $320 a month, or $3,840 yearly; Skip's cost $410 a month, or $4,920 annually. Over the course of 40 years, Bill will save $43,200 by paying $153,600 for insurance compared to $196,800 spent by Skip.

- **AUTO INSURANCE:** Though both own cars of an identical year, make, and model, Bill's insurance for his Lexus costs $1,800 a year, while Skip's runs $2,340. Bill's five-year savings on auto insurance is $2,700 ($9,000 paid by Bill versus $11,700 paid by Skip). Over 35 years, Bill's savings add up to $18,900.

A Promotion Won—Then Lost

All told, Bill saves at least $413,000 because of his lifetime of perfect credit. That's nearly a half-million dollars that Bill keeps in his bank account, simply because he pays his bills on time. But the financial

benefits don't end there. Bill and Skip are also up for the same job promotion—senior vice president of sales. Bill tossed his hat in the ring
for the promotion not knowing that Skip was going to go for it. When
Bill found out that Skip was interested in the job, Bill thought about
withdrawing his name. "The truth of the matter is that you are the
better salesman," Bill told Skip, adding, "Everyone knows you're a
shoo-in for the promotion because of your outstanding sales record.
You deserve a promotion."

As it turns out, the boss saw it that way too. After interviewing four
candidates up for the job, the boss picked Skip. But because the job
paid $100,000 annually, the human resources department performed
its customary background check, running Skip's credit report in the
process. Within 24 hours, Skip's job promotion had been rescinded.
The high-paying job ultimately went to Bill, who received a $25,000
raise—all because he paid his bills on time and had perfect credit and
Skip didn't. Neither guy thought it was fair, but as Skip's boss said
upon withdrawing the job promotion: "Hey, it's nothing personal. It's
just business." Apparently, the company figured that bad credit meant
that Skip wouldn't be as trustworthy and might be tempted to steal
customer funds if his own money problems worsened. Skip went
home seething mad. He consulted a lawyer to see if his boss could
legally offer him a job, and then take the job back just because of his
bad credit. The attorney advised Skip that unfortunately what the
employer had done was perfectly legal. When Bill went home, he was
ecstatic. He did the math and realized that over the next 25 years, the
extra $25,000 in salary he'd get from the promotion meant he'd gen-
erate $625,000 in additional income before retirement—not including
any other raises. As you can see, paying his bills on time allowed Bill
to save and earn a total of $1,038,100 more than poor Skip, who kept
skipping payments and wound up getting constantly penalized for his
lousy credit.

Good Credit Isn't Good Enough

Some of you might be asking, "Why do I need perfect credit? Isn't good credit good enough?" Simply put, the answer is no. If you've got horrendous credit, then by all means upgrading to good credit would be a major improvement. But why stop there? The difference between having good credit and perfect credit is like the difference between getting a 1100 on the SAT and scoring a perfect 1600. While 1100 is a good enough score to get into many schools, imagine the college prospects for those students who earned that 1600. Virtually every university admissions office in the country would vie to recruit them, offering college tours, extending generous financial aid packages or scholarships—in short, doing every- **Good credit isn't** thing in their power to sign those top-tier students. **good enough.**

Sometimes it's nice to be sought after like that. And consumers who have A-1 credit are the most sought after on the planet. I don't care if you're in Dallas, Texas, or Durban, South Africa. When you manage your credit wisely, you're in the driver's seat. Are you ready to rev up your engine and get this perfect credit that I've described? In the pages that follow, I'll give you the keys—figuratively speaking, of course—to your very own dream car. And, trust me, when you've got spectacular credit, the ride is superb. After all, when you're traveling first class, getting there is half the fun.

Seven Steps To Perfect Credit

What would you say if I told you there was a way you could you systematically develop perfect credit? There are seven foolproof steps you can use to develop perfect credit, strengthen your credit standing, and avoid the hassles and aggravation of having bad credit. Here's what you need to do to follow my PERFECT credit seven-step system:

P—Pull your credit report and FICO score regularly.

E—Examine your credit file thoroughly.

R—Reduce debt and manage bills wisely.

F—Fix errors and protect your credit.

E—Enhance your credit file constantly.

C—Contact creditors and negotiate.

T—Take time to frequently reevaluate your options.

STEP 1: PULL YOUR CREDIT REPORT AND FICO SCORE REGULARLY

When I coach people about their finances, one of the things I always recommend they do is to pull their credit report and check their FICO score routinely. Thanks to a relatively new law, called the FACT Act, consumers nationwide have the right to get their credit reports free of charge once a year. Simply log onto www.annualcreditreport.com. You can also get your credit report directly from each of the "big three" credit bureaus: Equifax, Experian, and TransUnion. Their addresses, phone numbers, and Web site appear at the end of this book. Additionally, you can log on to Fair Isaac's consumer Web site, www.myfico.com, and get all three credit reports along with your FICO scores. FICO scores, though, are not free. As of this writing, it cost $45 to obtain your FICO scores. Despite the cost, I think this is the preferred route because Fair Isaac provides a range of credit-related tools and information to help you boost your credit scores. Financial institutions rely on Fair Isaac too.

You can't improve your credit if you don't know where you stand.

While there are several different types of credit scores throughout the financial world, including the new VantageScore unveiled by the "big three" in 2006, 98 percent of credit card companies and 75 percent of mortgage lenders use FICO credit scores as the basis for their lending decisions.

Pulling your credit report and FICO score might seem like an obvious thing to do if you want to make an investment in yourself and start enhancing your credit reputation. However, I encounter a surprisingly large number of people who have never seen their credit report and for some reason don't want to. Some people are scared of what their credit file might show. They recall, for example, being turned down for a credit card, so they're imagining the worst. Well, no matter how bad things might be, ignoring a sickly credit file won't fix it, any more than ignoring a broken arm would fix that bone. You can't improve your credit if you don't know where you stand. So if you don't get your credit report and FICO score online today, mark a date on your calendar when you will do so. Then get into the habit of checking it regularly—meaning at least once a year. Don't wait until you're in the market for a mortgage or an auto loan. Get that credit report and FICO score now.

STEP 2: EXAMINE YOUR CREDIT FILE THOROUGHLY

Once you get your credit report, it's up to you to interpret the information; this can sometimes be confusing. You may notice that there are differences among the three different credit reports. For instance, perhaps there's a charge account on one report that isn't showing up on the other two. Or maybe the last mortgage on your old house is showing a balance when it should be reported as being paid off. At this point, you want to get a snapshot of how you are viewed by the rest of the lending and financial world. Are there any negative items listed such as late payments? What about public documents such as liens or judgments against you? These are obviously big red flags that hurt your credit reputation considerably. Or perhaps you have lots of accounts with small balances. In the eyes of some lenders, that may be a negative because having too much access to credit means you could go out and run up a boatload of bills.

If you've gotten your credit reports and FICO score from Fair Isaac, the most important thing for you to do at this point is to read the company's analysis of why your credit score is a certain number. Beyond late payments and other delinquencies, some other reasons that your FICO score may take a hit are if you have too much debt outstanding, if you have too many recently opened accounts, or if you have a high number of credit inquiries. According to Fair Isaac, there are five criteria that go into formulating your credit score:

1. Your payment history makes up 35 percent of your FICO score.
2. The amount of debt owed comprises 30 percent.
3. Length of credit history accounts for 15 percent.
4. The existence of new credit alone makes up 10 percent.
5. The type of credit being used constitutes the final 10 percent.

Here is my own assessment of credit ranking, based solely on your FICO score and my personal and professional dealings with bankers and lenders of all kinds:

IF YOUR FICO SCORE IS...	THEN YOUR CREDIT IS:
760–850	Perfect
759–700	Good
699–650	Average
649–620	So-so
619 and below	Poor

Note that for many financial institutions, 620 is somewhat of a magic cutoff number. For example, many banks will require you to have a FICO score of at least 620 in order to get a decent mortgage rate. If your score is lower than 620, can you still get the loan? Yes, in most cases. But, depending on the severity of your credit problems, you should expect to pay a lot higher interest and more finance charges over the life of the loan than you would if your score was above 620. That's true at every level of the credit spectrum. Those in the perfect credit range will pay less than those with good credit; those with good credit will get better terms than people with average credit, and so on.

STEP 3: REDUCE DEBT AND MANAGE BILLS WISELY

As I mentioned earlier, there is a very strong link between your debt and your credit standing. Because your payment history—or how good you are at paying your bills on time—is the number one factor in determining your FICO score, it's imperative that you take managing your debt very seriously. Start by doing whatever it takes to never, ever miss a payment—for any reason whatsoever. If you do that one single thing, you will start to raise your FICO score. If you've skipped or made late payments in the past because money was tight, you need to adjust your budget to ensure that you faithfully pay every single bill on time. (Check back in Chapter 1 for budgeting strategies). And when I say "every bill," I mean exactly that. Don't neglect your electric bill, in the mistaken belief that a local energy service won't report your delinquent account to the credit bureaus. It can—and it will.

The same is true for cell phone providers, gas, electric, and water companies. Don't believe for one minute that the only bills you have to keep up to date to protect your credit are your mortgage, car loan, and credit cards. A 30-day late payment, regardless of what it is for, hurts your credit report. Would you believe that, in some parts of the

> **Perfect credit is something you should constantly strive for, and managing your bills diligently is the chief way to accomplish this.**

country, even parking tickets and overdue library fines are being reported to credit bureaus? It's true. Can you imagine being denied a bank loan or having to get one at a higher rate, just because of a fine you got for failing to promptly return a library book? As I said in the beginning, perfect credit is something you should constantly strive for, and managing your bills diligently is the chief way to accomplish this.

In addition to being judicious about paying current bills, getting serious about knocking out long-standing debt will go a long way in boosting your financial reputation and enhancing your credit standing. Many of you have read one of my previous books, called *Zero Debt: The Ultimate Guide to Financial Freedom*. If so, you know that I consider excessive debt to be a financial cancer; it's the worst economic plague with which you'll probably ever have to wrestle. In Chapter 3 of this book, I reveal a number of proven strategies for eliminating debt, but for now let me highlight two things you can do that will simultaneously reduce consumer debt, save money, and more quickly upgrade your credit standing.

The first is to use a home-equity loan to pay off the balances on your credit cards. The second is to shift balances from high-rate credit cards to those with lower interest rates. Getting a home-equity loan or an equity line of credit can be a smart strategy for a few reasons. The interest rate on home-equity loans (currently in the 6 percent range) is far less than what you're probably paying on your credit cards (likely in the 15 percent plus range). Additionally, the interest on home-equity loans is tax deductible; the interest levied on your credit cards is not. Finally, from a credit-scoring standpoint, mortgage debt is treated more favorably than credit card debt, so converting that consumer debt is likely to positively affect your FICO score.

The second is shifting debt from one credit card to another. This may be more art than science, but, done properly, it can also save you lots of money and keep you from hurting your FICO score. I tell you more about this in Chapter 3.

STEP 4: FIX ERRORS AND PROTECT YOUR CREDIT

Consumer groups estimate that 70 percent of all credit reports have mistakes in them. That's an awful lot of misinformation—and it could be costing you money. If you have errors in your credit file and you're in the market for a loan, you could wind up paying a lot more in interest than you rightfully should. Mistakes happen for a lot of reasons. Sometimes there's an inputting error by a clerk who erroneously types something, like the spelling of your name, and then you get confused with someone else. Or maybe one of the digits in your social security number is inadvertently transposed, and inaccurate information starts to be reported about you. In other cases, family members have found that their credit files somehow get mistakenly comingled.

For instance, Fred Jones, Jr., might find that his credit report lists some accounts that belong to his father, Fred Jones, Sr. Whatever the cause, mistakes in your credit report should be dealt with as soon as you discover them. Each credit bureau has a dispute resolution process that requires you to you write a letter to the credit agency and state what information is inaccurate **Seventy percent of all credit reports have mistakes in them.** or incomplete in your credit file. Under the Fair Credit Reporting Act, the credit bureau has 30 days to investigate your claims and notify you of the results. Writing the credit bureaus is typically most effective when there is identity confusion, when personal information about you is listed incorrectly, or when your file contains completely wrong data—such as an account you never opened.

But let's say that you find an error based on misinformation that was supplied by one of your creditors. This would be the case if you:

- Closed an account, yet the account still shows that it's open.
- Are reported as paying late, but you actually made your payment on time.
- Paid off an account, but your credit report still shows a balance.

In all these instances, it's best to contact the source of the information and ask the source to fix the report. If it's a legitimate error, without much to dispute, the company will readily address the problem. Even if it has to do its own investigation—perhaps because your claim is not cut-and-dried—it's usually better to start with the cred- itor. The reason is that when you dispute something with the credit bureau, its information may get changed, but then the next month it's possible that the error could reappear in your credit file. Errors that are disputed and resolved at the creditor level are far more likely to remain off of your credit report.

Updates to your credit file usually take about 30 to 45 days to hap- pen. However, if you're in the market for a mortgage, you can have mistakes in your credit report fixed in as little as 48 hours through a process called "credit rescoring." It allows mortgage bankers to sub- mit proof of a mistake in your credit file directly to the credit agencies. In turn, those agencies give your file priority status and quickly update your credit information electronically. This way, an error in your credit file doesn't cost you money or jeopardize your chance to get that mortgage.

To enhance your credit reputation, you also need to guard your- self against identity theft—the fastest-growing white-collar crime in the country. Unfortunately, identity theft affects up to 10 million Americans each year, as crooks get increasingly sophisticated and more determined in their efforts to target new victims. Some identity thieves use online "phishing" scams to get you to divulge private infor- mation; but others use decidedly low-tech methods like stealing your wallet or dumpster-diving to obtain credit card numbers and other information about you. To prevent identity theft, shred sensitive doc- uments before discarding them, and never carry your Social Security card with you.

You should also consider purchasing identity theft insurance. A handful of insurance companies nationwide offer this coverage. Since the average victim of identity theft spends about 200 hours and $1,000 cleaning up the mess brought on by this heinous crime, identity theft insurance reimburses you for a range of things like attorney's fees, phone bills, and time lost from your job. Coverage usually goes up to around $25,000.

If you are the victim of identity theft, alert the credit bureaus (so they can put a notice in your credit files), notify your local police department, contact the Federal Trade Commission (877-ID-THEFT or www.ftc.gov), and seek help from the Identity Theft Resource Center (858-693-7935 or www.idtheftresource.org) in San Diego.

STEP 5: ENHANCE YOUR CREDIT FILE CONSTANTLY

The experts at Fair Isaac say that paying your bills promptly results in a positive payment record, which is the top factor in calculating your FICO score. When you keep those accounts open and their status is good, over time you also create a lengthy credit history, another factor in your FICO score. But there are a number of other little-known ways to improve your credit standing.

The first method is by adding positive information to your credit file. Up until now, you've learned how to pull your credit reports, examine them, and fix any errors. Now it's time to get proactive about what's contained in your credit file. The information that you and others currently see is based on information creditors have provided about you. But what you have to say does count for something. And, if you're smart, you'll augment your credit file to put yourself in the best possible light. For example, if you notice that a mortgage you paid off appears on one credit report but not on others, you should write to those two credit agencies and ask them to add that information to your credit file. It doesn't matter that the account is no longer open or has a zero balance. To lenders and others who view your credit file paying off a previous mortgage is a significant accomplishment and a positive sign—even if it was from selling or refinancing the house. The idea is to show that you have a track record of managing a financial obligation. If you see that your home address is incorrectly listed or that your job of 10 years is omitted from your credit file, then that too is something you should have added to the report. Your address and job information aren't taken into consideration for the purposes of computing your FICO credit score; however, most creditors and lenders will look carefully at that information to determine how stable you are and therefore how much of a risk you are financially. Student loans that were paid off—but that are not showing up—represent another category of positive items you should add to your credit report.

If you're close to someone who has excellent credit, you can also use piggybacking to boost your credit standing. In piggybacking you essentially share credit history with someone who has a better credit rating than you do. For instance, that person might cosign a small personal loan or add you on as a card holder on a credit card he or she has used and paid faithfully for years. Piggybacking gives you the benefit of someone else's great credit standing. You have to make sure, though, that the creditor in question reports the information to the credit bureaus separately in your name, and not just in that person's name. Also, don't mess up here. It's one thing to foul up your own credit. But if someone else goes out on a limb for you to help you establish or restore your credit rating, you owe it to that person to pay the bill as agreed so you don't end up damaging his or her credit reputation.

Last, for those of you who are just establishing credit, there is more good news. In the past, in order to get a credit rating going, you had to go into debt—by applying for and using a credit card, obtaining an auto loan, or getting a mortgage. Now there's a new way to establish credit and demonstrate fiscal responsibility without going into debt. A service called PRBC (Payment Reporting Builds Credit) lets students, the newly divorced, immigrants, women, minorities, and others prove their creditworthiness by tracking their habits at making timely payments for rent, utilities, and other recurring bills. This is a huge market: an estimated 50 million people don't have enough traditional payment history in order to have a standard credit file, according to Fair Isaac. If you're caught in a catch-22 and you can't get credit because you have no credit history, then build your credit history by logging on to www.prbc.com. It's a voluntary service and one that I believe could be worthwhile for many individuals.

STEP 6: CONTACT CREDITORS AND NEGOTIATE

A crucial step in achieving perfect credit involves getting creditors and bill collectors to work with you when you've had past financial problems. You can greatly enhance your credit standing if you could get late payments and other blemishes deleted from your credit file. The way to do this is to call up your creditors and negotiate. Ironically, when your account is past due, that's the time you're in the best position of all to negotiate. You have something the creditors or bill collectors wants—cash. They also have something you want—the power to update your credit report. So your strategy, in a nutshell, should be to dangle the cash carrot before their eyes. Depending on the status of your account (open, closed, charged-off, etc.) and how far behind you are in your payments, your goal should be to bring your account current, to set up a payment plan, or to agree on a reduced amount that the company will accept in lieu of full payment. In all these cases, what you're really doing is settling your account and restoring it to good standing. In exchange for doing that, you must insist on getting the creditor or bill collectors' agreement to delete negative information that was previously reported about you. At the very least, they should update their records to reflect a "paid" current status. But often creditors will do this, while making such notations in your credit file as "was 60 days late." Therefore, in most cases, it's best to firmly negotiate for the outright elimination of negative information in your credit report.

Firmly negotiate for the outright elimination of negative information in your credit report.

When you reach an agreement, put it in writing and have both sides sign the pact before you pay a dime. This way you're protecting yourself if the person you're negotiating with reneges on your deal.

STEP 7: TAKE TIME TO FREQUENTLY REEVALUATE YOUR OPTIONS

In your quest to achieve and maintain perfect credit, it's imperative that you re-assess your credit life from time to time. This entails scrutinizing the terms of your current credit cards and loans, analyzing any new credit offers you may get, and planning for the unexpected. For instance, have any of your interest rates changed while you weren't paying attention? If they've been ratcheted up, because of no fault of your own, you'll want to call your creditors and negotiate for a lower rate. In other cases, you may find that your credit card company is implementing some new change with which you don't agree. It could be a switch in the financial terms or the company notifying you about its plans to sell or rent customer names to its marketing affiliates. If you object, you should write to voice your displeasure. It may be that you have to pay the card off or switch cards to avoid being subjected to terms you find onerous. Finally, just because you have a certain mortgage, line of credit or credit card today, doesn't mean that it will forever be the right product for you. Your needs may change, and maybe you no longer need a personal line of credit, for example.

The idea is to make sure that you current credit picture adequately reflects your needs. In doing so, you don't want to think exclusively about life in the "here and now." Be forward-thinking, and make sure you have the appropriate credit you might need for the future. Part of proper credit management involves planning for the unexpected and building in some wiggle room.

For instance, if your company starts laying off employees, and you've been notified that in 60 days you'll be getting a pink slip with no compensation package. Let's also assume that this downsizing couldn't have come at a worse time—because you spouse also just got axed, or maybe took ill and can't work. Under normal circumstances, I tell people to decline those insurance offers from credit card companies. But in this scenario, since you have some advance notice, it may well be worth your money to get that credit card insurance protection which allows you to forgo or reduce your credit card payments in the event of a job loss. This way, even if money gets especially tight, you can protect your credit standing.

I Have Perfect Credit—Now What?

We've looked extensively at how you can invest in yourself by improving your credit rating. In the financial world, lenders view your overall credit standing—as summed up by your FICO credit score—as a snapshot of the strength of your financial reputation. Beyond your credit score, though, there are other ways you can invest in yourself, enhance your reputation, and add money to your bank account in the process.

It Pays To Get A College Degree

Some of you reading this book have earned a college degree, but many of you have not. Nationwide, only one in four Americans has a four-year degree. If you are among those without a college degree, I'd strongly urge you to consider getting one. Obtaining a college education is a phenomenal investment in yourself because it substantially boosts your earnings potential. I say "potential," because nothing is guaranteed. A lot depends on what you do with that education.

Nonetheless, U.S. Census Bureau statistics show that people with Bachelor's degrees earn roughly 62 percent more per year than people with only high school diplomas. Over a lifetime, that translates into more than a $1 million earnings gap between the average college graduate and the average high school graduate.

> Having a college education is a phenomenal investment in yourself because it substantially boosts your earnings potential—people with Bachelor's degrees earn roughly 62 percent more per year than those without degrees.

MAKING COLLEGE AFFORDABLE

There's more financial aid available now than ever before—a record $129 billion in aid for students, to be precise. Roughly 60 percent of all college students receive grant aid. In 2004–2005, the latest period for which figures were available, grant aid averaged more than $3,300 for those attending public four-year colleges, and about $9,600 per student at private four-year colleges, according to the College Board. So even though we all hear a lot about the skyrocketing cost of a college education, when you take grants and other aid into consideration, your out-of-pocket costs are likely to be far less than the published figures for tuition and fees.

In your quest to get a four-year degree, nobody's saying that you must attend an expensive Ivy League school, where tuition is $30,000 or so annually. To overcome the dilemma of high-cost education, pick a lower-priced institution. These comprise the majority of schools nationwide anyway. Currently, about 60 percent of students attending four-year schools pay less than $6,000 for tuition and fees. Only about 2 percent of all students in the United States pay $33,000 or more in college tuition and fees, the College Board reports.

And don't forget about your benefits package at work. You may be fretting over college expenses for nothing if paid college tuition is one of the perks your employer offers. If your boss sees you as a valuable part of your corporate organization, chances are he or she will be glad to see you pursue your degree. Good bosses know that you'll be an even stronger asset to the company when you are a more educated worker—one who combines academic know-how with practical business savvy and experience.

Besides getting financial aid, attending a less expensive four-year institution, or getting your employer to pay for your degree, another smart solution to the affordability dilemma is to begin your college education by attending a two-year school where tuition and fees average $2,191. And since the typical two-year public college student receives about $1,800 in aid, that means you'd only have to come up with about $400 a year for tuition and fees. After you get your two-year diploma, then you can transfer to a four-year institution and obtain your Bachelor's degree. Completing your initial years of study at a two-year school allows you to save tremendously on your education, yet still make progress toward getting that four-year degree.

So no more excuses about being short on money. The truth of the matter is that if you want to earn that college degree, you'll figure out a way to make it work financially. Remember, getting that degree significantly bolsters your chances of becoming a millionaire, because you'll be able to leverage the earnings power of that degree and turn it into a lifetime of higher earnings.

FLEXIBLE COLLEGE OPTIONS ABOUND

For those of you who say that, with your already jam-packed schedule, there is just no way you that can possibly squeeze in college, I say you don't have to be in a regularly scheduled morning class or evening class. In fact, who says you have to *go* to class at all? Enrollment in distance-education courses is on the rise, as is enrollment in online classes. Right now, 33 percent of private four-year colleges and universities offer online degree programs, and 40 percent of them offer long-distance learning programs. At last count, these distance programs had 2.4 million students enrolled. You could be one of them, taking classes remotely and learning from the convenience of your own home. You can also pace yourself. There's no need to rush through your undergraduate or graduate degree program. Getting your college degree doesn't mean you're obligated to take a full course load. Unless you have extraordinarily flexible job hours, and limited personal and professional responsibilities, don't plan on attending school full time. About 40 percent of all undergraduate students in America are enrolled on a part-time basis, and you can adopt that strategy, too.

YOU'RE NEVER TOO OLD

Finally, are you wary about returning to college, or going for the first time, because you think you'll feel old and out of place? Well, I have a news flash for you. Gone are the days when the perky little 18-year-old typified the average college student in this country. The College Board notes that enrollment patterns have changed dramatically at most institutions of higher education. While individuals between the ages of 18 and 24 might represent the traditional full-time college student, far more of today's college students are nontraditional attendees. In 1970, 64 percent of college students were age 21 and younger, while only 6 percent were age 30 and older. Currently, only 47 percent are 21 and under; the 30-plus crowd now accounts for 23 percent of the student population.

So if you're an "older" student, I'm sure you could stand to be in a classroom where at least one out of four students is likely to be in your age bracket. If my Uncle Otis could do it, so can you. Uncle Otis returned to college when he was in his late 50s. I was greatly proud of him when he began studying political science. He did it for the love of education, and because he was interested in the subject. Also, after telling my sisters and me our whole lives about the importance of a college education, he figured he would offer us a living example of deeds matching words. By the way, I never once heard him complain about being the oldest in the class or that he was too old to attend school. At one point or another, I'm sure he may have thought it. But he certainly didn't let that "old" thinking hold him back.

In this chapter so far, I've emphasized the two best investments you can make in yourself to strengthen your financial reputation: strengthening your credit and obtaining a college degree. I want to also highlight the other four ways in which you can invest in yourself. Remember, this is part of my SIMPLE strategy:

S —Strive for perfect credit.

I —Improve your education.

M—Make it a lifelong endeavor to increase your knowledge, training, and skills.

P —Put money in your own business before anyone else's.

L —Learn to give back.

E —Earn more by creating stability in your personal and professional life.

Grow Intellectually, Flourish Financially

We've already discussed how earning a college degree can be a million-dollar move. Now, I want to tell you how to further jumpstart your earnings capacity—through continuous learning. When you expand your knowledge base, you not only grow intellectually, but you flourish financially as well. Remember that million-dollar earnings gap between high school graduates and those with college degrees? Well, even if you choose not to enroll in a degree program, you can still improve your chances of becoming a millionaire by constantly upgrading your skills and abilities. No matter what your chosen profession, there are books you can read to learn the latest trends in your industry, classes you can take to update your knowledge, and training programs you can enter to augment your practical, hands-on experience. Continual learning is all about never resting on your laurels. It's about realizing that no matter how much education or experience you might currently have, there's always something new to discover: some new technique, some new theory, some new application—something that will help you in your chosen profession, or perhaps inspire you to change professions.

Savvy millionaires aren't know-it-alls. They embrace the concept of continuous education. I hope you too will open your mind to the enormous possibilities inherent in lifelong learning. If you do, I'm sure you'll find that the benefits of an ongoing education are immeasurable. When you are a lifelong learner, you don't just update your skills set by learning specific how-to aspects of your current job. You also become more marketable in the workplace by enhancing your communication skills, problem-solving skills, analytical and critical thinking skills, individual and teamwork skills, technological skills, as well as management and leadership skills. All these traits are highly desirable in today's workforce—and employers are often willing to pay top dollar to attract talented people who possess these skills. While it is almost universally recognized that ongoing learning is important, participation in lifelong learning activities is actually low, experts say. This means that most of us are giving lip service to this idea. We say we know it's important; but then we take no action to incorporate continuous learning into our lives. Don't fall into that trap.

The Entrepreneur as Millionaire

I realize that a good number of you may not be working for anyone else; you may be entrepreneurs who run your own business. If that's the case for you, you likely already know that statistics show that as many as two-thirds of today's current millionaires are self-employed. In fact, one study of 1,000 millionaires found that 80 percent are first-generation wealthy. The average small business owner has an annual household income of about $135,000 and assets topping the $1 million mark. That's a strong financial incentive for those of you considering launching your own business. According to a 2005 survey conducted by Harris Interactive, nearly 50 percent of all American adults would like to start a business.

Starting your own business is one of the strongest votes of confidence you can give yourself.

If you want to leave corporate America and be your own boss, finding the money to get your enterprise off the ground may be your primary concern. While many entrepreneurs initially finance their operations through personal lines of credit, credit cards, or loans from family and friends, you can seek other funding sources. If you qualify, there's traditional bank financing to launch your operations, purchase inventory, or pay for advertising. Loans from the Small Business Administration are also available for start-up companies. And don't forget to check out angel investors, venture capitalists, or microenterprise lenders who might be willing to supply you with capital.

The Association for Enterprise Opportunity defines a microenterprise as a sole proprietorship, partnership, or family business that has fewer than five employees, that is generally too small to obtain commercial banking services, and that requires $35,000 or less in start-up capital. You can also get free advice and assistance in creating a business plan from Small Business Development Centers nationwide, and from groups like SCORE, the Service Corps of Retired Executives. No matter what your interest, as long as you do your homework and find that there's a legitimate market for the product or service you wish to sell, being a small business owner can definitely smooth your pathway to millionaire's row.

Starting your own business is one of the strongest votes of confidence you can give yourself. By investing in your own business —especially before you pour money into anyone else's enterprise— you tell the world that you value yourself, your special abilities, and your ability to create your own wealth. When you manage your business well, you also enhance your reputation by providing your customers with great products or service. Two quick caveats for aspiring entrepreneurs: research potential business ideas carefully before settling on your final plans. And by all means, avoid putting money into get-rich-quick schemes. As any honest entrepreneur will tell you, generating wealth from your own business is not an overnight proposition. As a small business owner myself, I know from first-hand experience that running a business is fun, personally rewarding, and intellectually stimulating. But it also involves a lot of hard work, long hours, and uncertainty. If you can stomach the risk, though, the ride is definitely worthwhile.

You've Got To Give To Get

It might seem counterintuitive to suggest that you give to others as a way to invest in yourself, but that's exactly what I recommend. You see, financially fit millionaires—and even millionaires in training—are a blessing to those around them. They help others in need. They share what they have, and not begrudgingly, either. We've all heard the Bible verse proclaiming that "you reap what you sow." I believe that wholeheartedly. Indeed, I've received so many blessings in my life (financial and otherwise) that I know beyond a doubt that the more you give out, and the more you put into something, the more you get back. Many of us are brainwashed into thinking that the only way we can give is to donate monetarily. But you can actually donate your time, talent, expertise, or even physical labor to individuals, organizations, or causes you want to support. True philanthropists do this all the time, and build up their reputation in the process. Even if you don't subscribe to the biblical principle of tithing and giving back 10 percent of your income, you probably believe in karma, even without realizing it. Have you ever uttered a phrase such as: "What goes around comes around"? If so, this demonstrates your subconscious acknowledgement that the world operates according to a certain level of give and take. I'm not suggesting at all that any of you should help another person in need just to get something back. That would be a selfish and wrong-headed way of trying to invest in yourself. But when you can honestly, selflessly give of yourself—just for the joy of giving—that's when you'll find your generosity returned many times over. Try it and see.

Stability Is Not Boring

As a Money Coach, I often make television appearances to teach individuals and families nationwide about how to better manage their finances. Once, when I was a guest expert on the TV show *Dr. Phil,* one of the people on the program was a woman named Lynette (ironic, I know). Well, Lynette was an admitted shopaholic who was nearly $38,000 in debt. She shopped whenever she wanted, and said she really didn't look at price tags. She also admitted that her free-spending ways were straining her marriage and setting a bad example for her teenage daughters. "We live like millionaires," Lynette said. Clearly, they were far from being true millionaires—in terms of mindset or net worth. What I found most troubling about Lynette was her constant need for change. This woman had bought ten cars in five years and had also moved several times during that period. She said she got bored easily with her purchases, and wanted nicer cars and homes. I don't think she recognized how that kind of change created unnecessary upheaval in her family's life.

Maintaining order and stability in your world is a powerful way of investing in your reputation.

While I offered Lynette a number of debt-reduction tips, in retrospect, I wish I had told her what I'm telling you now: you can do yourself a big favor by creating stability in your personal and professional life. Maintaining order and stability in your world is a powerful way of investing in your reputation. Yet it's something that most people overlook. I hope that you won't though, because you'll generate and keep more money, earn more respect, and greatly improve your standing in the financial world if you can cultivate an air of stability around you.

Think about how bankers and others view you when you're constantly changing important things—like your home telephone number or your place of residence. It just doesn't look good. Why do you think it is that loan applications often ask how long you've lived at your present location, or how long you've worked at a certain job? The bank is looking for stability. Longevity is a sign that you're settled and will be responsible in meeting your financial obligations. The same theory is held by employers. When you apply for a job, prospective bosses want to know how long you've been at your previous workplace. It's great to have career advancement and to learn new things. But switching companies every year and engaging in constant job hopping is unattractive to most employers because it does not indicate a stable track record. To create stability in your universe, consider implementing these ideas:

- **QUIT CHANGING JOBS FREQUENTLY:** If your current position is not challenging or does not paying enough, first consider whether you can get promoted within your current firm, instead of hopping to another company.

- **AVOID THE URGE TO SWAP CARS EVERY YEAR OR TWO:** Remember that every time you buy a car it depreciates in value the minute you drive it off the lot. Besides, a lot of people "upgrading" their automobiles are doing it primarily for image and to keep up with the Joneses. Don't bother.

■ **MAINTAIN CONTINUITY IN YOUR RESIDENCE ADDRESS AND OTHER CONTACT INFO:** As mentioned, in the financial world, bankers look for stability in your home life. Every time I try to call, message, or write some people, I have to double-check to see if they have the same phone number, e-mail address, or street address. Trust me: your relatives, friends, and associates may not tell you to your face, but they'd appreciate some continuity in your life. Behind your back, they're probably murmuring about how you've "moved again."

■ **DON'T LET YOUR LOVE LIFE BECOME A REVOLVING DOOR:** Realize that breakups are expensive. They can take their toll in a number of ways. Divorce is financially costly—not to mention emotionally painful. Unfortunately, I've been through a divorce. And in the process, one of the interesting statistics I learned was that, whenever a couple divorces, assuming it takes a year to go through the court proceedings, the economic recovery period is two and a half years, as each party adjusts to the costs of running two households instead of one. If a divorce drags on for two years, then it typically takes five years for the parties involved to recover financially. You should also realize that instability in your personal life can also have a much longer and much more severe impact on your personal finances. For instance, if you split with your spouse, depending on your individual circumstances and the state in which you live, you just may have to fork over half of your assets that took years to build, like 401(k) monies, real estate and other property.

So please don't think that being stable is boring. Having some degree of permanence, or at least longevity, will actually put you in good financial stead—and help you avoid a lot of unnecessary drama.

In summary, investing first last and always in your own reputation offers unlimited opportunities for wealth-building and personal satisfaction. Whether it's achieving perfect credit, improving your education and skills, or fostering stability in your personal world— all these things literally put (or keep) millions of dollars in your bank account and give you access to a world of financial and nonfinancial benefits.

You are the ultimate blue-chip investment.

While some might argue that investing in stocks and bonds is your best bet for creating a fortune, investing in the financial markets is just that: a bet. And unfortunately, the vast majority of people don't get it right. Rationally speaking, there is unquestionably the chance to amass great riches through traditional investing. The problem, though, is that investors rarely behave rationally. They frequently allow emotions such as fear or greed to govern their actions. In the end, they often wind up making a host of mistakes that diminish their wealth. I don't believe it has to be that way. Nor do I believe you should forgo making traditional investments. It's just that you need a proper road map, and you have to know which pitfalls to avoid along the way. I discuss investing in the stock market at length in Chapter 5, sharing insights to help you become a successful investor. But if you can see yourself as the ultimate blue-chip investment and follow the guidance I've just outlined, I'm confident that you've got the proper mindset to become a millionaire many times over.

3

LIVE LIKE A LENDER,
NOT A BORROWER

M any of you are sabotaging your own efforts to become millionaires by your financial conduct, especially your spending
decisions. In this chapter, you will take a closer look at what you owe
and the causes for your debt. You will also determine your own particular money personality. From these exercises you will glean valuable
insights into your own money habits, discover how to break unhealthy
financial behaviors, and find out why you may be overspending,
spending impulsively, or sometimes spending for all the wrong reasons. All these misdirected activities result in one big financial
calamity: excessive debt. To our peril, we've evolved into a nation of
debtors. In previous generations, cash used to be king. Nowadays,
however, we live on credit. We use it to buy everything from cars to
homes. Then we use credit again to buy more stuff to fill those cars
and homes.

The average U.S. household has $9,300 in credit card debt, accord-
ing to CardWeb. The National Automobile Dealers Association says
that the average new car purchased in America cost more than
$28,000 and is financed over five years. All told, typical national debt

totals roughly 107 percent of an individual's income. This means that if you earn $50,000 a year, chances are you owe that amount and then some. Collectively, household consumer debt has topped $2 trillion in the United States. Nearly $1 trillion of that is attributable to credit card debt. Another $8 trillion is owed in mortgages. I suppose the millions of indebted individuals and families have taken their cues from the nation's corporate giants and the political establishment, because they're in debt too. In the aggregate, America owes a whopping $20 trillion—including individual household debt, business IOUs and government liabilities. What's driving all this borrowing—and spending—at the consumer level?

> **In the United States, household consumer debt has topped $2 trillion.**

There are many reasons behind the phenomenon. For starters, we live in a consumer culture that glorifies things and encourages us to want more stuff that will purportedly make us happier. Additionally, many people have the mentality that instant gratification is far more desirable than long-term satisfaction. Our widespread debt is certainly also driven by banks and other lenders who make access to credit easier than ever—often at a higher price than ever, of course.

Financial Education Gets Lip Service

All these reasons undoubtedly play a role in our mushrooming debt load. But if I had to point to the single biggest cause of this nation's out-of-control debt, I'd cite a shameful lack of financial literacy. It's abhorrent to think that we educate kids about all manner of hazardous scenarios they will face in life—from peer pressure to smoke or use drugs to the dangers of talking to strangers—yet we largely ignore the perils of mismanaging money and credit. Some suggest that credit cards are so potent that they should come with their own warning labels. If that's the case, the best early warning system we can create is to teach young people about how treacherous it is to be mired in debt and to mismanage their finances.

Financial education should be emphasized in schools from the elementary level through college. Certainly, a host of entities nationwide offer tremendously valuable financial education initiatives. I'm thinking of the Jump$tart Coalition, the Money Savvy Generation, the National Endowment for Financial Education (www.nefe.org), the National Council on Economic Education (www.ncee.net), and a handful of others. But these programs barely touch the surface concerning what we should be doing to make financial literacy an integral part of the curriculum for every student in this country—beginning in early childhood. For the most part, schools give lip service to the idea of educating young people about proper money management. As a result, financially illiterate young people turn into financially illiterate, financially irresponsible adults.

> **Financially illiterate young people turn into financially illiterate, financially irresponsible adults.**

I could recount a litany of areas in which the average adult consumer is lacking in basic economic knowledge and skills. What is most hurtful to the typical consumer is that the majority of people don't comprehend the magnitude of their spending decisions, particularly as they pertain to making purchases on credit. So many people think it's perfectly acceptable to pay for things over time that we now charge everything from $8 meals at fast food restaurants to IRS tax payments.

Behind the Eight Ball

What most people don't recognize is that living the life of a borrower means that they're always behind the eight ball, continually paying two to three times the list price for purchases. Snagged a nice 50-inch plasma TV "on sale for just $999" at your favorite electronics store? Well, if you bought it with a MasterCard and pay for it over time, that

$999 becomes more like $3,000. Got a new gold watch for 500 bucks using your Visa card? It may not be as appealing when you realize that

Live like a lender, not like a borrower.

your beloved timepiece really costs $1,500—and although it may stop ticking, the bill you owe for it won't.

Operating as a habitual borrower is detrimental in many other ways too. Freewheeling spending and acceptance of easy credit has turned the average consumer into a financial time bomb. Being a habitual borrower has many of you only two paychecks away from financial disaster. To combat the debt curse, you must change your thinking and your behavior. Specifically, it's imperative that you begin to live like a lender, not a borrower.

What does a lender do?

- Loans money (mainly to the right borrowers).
- Rejects loans from questionable borrowers.
- Collects interest.
- Gathers money and assets.
- Manages risk.
- Earns profits.

What does a borrower do?

- Borrows money (often from the wrong lenders).
- Approves loans to questionable borrowers.
- Pays interest.
- Spends money and assets.
- Assumes risk.
- Suffers losses.

Even a quick glance tells you that it's far more advantageous to be a lender than a borrower. Let's take a closer look at the benefits and drawbacks of each—after all, these financial lending institutions rake in billions of dollars in profits each year. For the savvy Millionaire-in-Training, there are some lessons to be learned about how these institutions operate. It

> "The borrower is servant to the lender." —Proverbs 22:7

seems they've taken a key lesson from the Bible—and so should we. Proverbs 22:7 says: "Just as the rich rule the poor, so the borrower is servant to the lender."

Lending Money with Discretion

It may be stating the obvious but one of the chief functions of a lender is to lend money—but that is too simplistic a definition of the lender's role. A more accurate description of what the lender is doing is lending money *to the right people.* The fact is, lenders don't arbitrarily lend money; they don't lend money just because they're asked, and they don't lend money to people they believe are highly unlikely to repay their loans. Instead, savvy lenders establish preset criteria to determine to whom they will lend money. They minimize their risks by screening out those deemed unworthy from a credit standpoint. No job and no income? Chances are you'll get no loan—at least not a traditional one or one with favorable terms. Have bad credit and a history of failing to repay your debts? Again, the odds are you'll be denied a standard loan. Or you'll be required to put up collateral to secure the loan.

In addition to loaning money and managing customer risk, lenders also accept deposits. They use these deposits to their advantage because having a large amount of assets under their management gives them the financial wherewithal to make loans and perform other functions. Lenders understand that by making loans, collecting interest on those loans, charging fees for a variety of services, and managing risk, they will directly affect the bottom line, resulting in a profit or loss for the organization. In most cases, as mentioned, the lending business is highly profitable.

Borrowing Money Indiscriminately

What about the borrower, that is the consumer? What does he or she do? Well, again, if I may state the obvious, the borrower borrows money. In most cases, people borrow money indiscriminately, accepting a slew of credit card offers that comes their way—by telephone, in the mail, or in person. A consumer who signs up for a department store credit card for the instant 10 percent discount—and then pays that balance over time—is blind to the fact that any discount received is wiped out many times over by the finance charges imposed.

Some people borrow from the wrong sources—like payday lenders who charge sky-high interest rates. Most individuals take very little care in scrutinizing the source of funds; just as long as easy money or credit is to be had, the borrower is willing to sign on the dotted line. Because of their poor financial habits, borrowers are in the position of constantly paying interest instead of earning or collecting interest. They also assume exorbitant amounts of risk, by taking on too much debt and underestimating the possibility that something could go wrong. And then when a job loss, a sudden illness, or a car accident occurs—anything unexpected that jeopardizes the borrower's ability to repay his or her loan—losses result. Losses in the form of late fees, higher interest charges, stress, and tarnished credit.

The Wrong Side of the Deal

From a pure business standpoint, do you know why borrowers seem to remain forever in debt? It's because they're on the wrong side of the deal. Most of us accept the fact that, in any transaction, there are two sides to the deal. On Wall Street, whenever someone wants to sell a stock, the deal doesn't get done until that seller (or his or her broker) finds a willing buyer. Once that's accomplished, then the transaction takes place. There's a meeting of the minds. Both sides agree on a

price. One person effectively says, "Okay, I'm ready to sell my stock, and I'm offering it at $45 a share." Then the other individual basically says, "Okay, I want to buy that stock, and I'm willing to purchase it for $45 a share." The deal is done. In the lending arena, the same thing happens millions of times each day.

> **Every time you use credit, you're agreeing to play the role of the borrower.**

Whether you realize it or not, every time you use credit, you're agreeing to play the role of the borrower, and the bank or credit card company involved is acting as the lender. And, as the borrower, you're accepting what the credit card company is offering. So if that company is charging you 29 percent interest to use your credit card and you go for it, then you're essentially saying, "Okay, I'm willing to borrow money from you at the 29 percent rate you're offering."

This relationship, more often than not, proves costly to the borrower and lucrative to the lender. Some of you may be saying: Wait a minute, credit card companies sometimes lose money, and they also lend to high-risk borrowers all the time, especially those that target so-called subprime borrowers. It's true that subprime lending represents a portion of some lenders' financial activities. But it's also true that, with billions of dollars at their disposal, they can afford to take on this kind of repayment risk. As proof, consider this: credit card delinquencies hit an all-time high in 2005. The two sides to this story are that (1) consumers had a whopping amount of debt that they couldn't pay off, and (2) those delinquent accounts—about 3 percent of accounts—still amounted to only a relatively small amount of losses for lenders. In fact, as part of their business model, lenders factor in a certain amount of losses, because they know they'll have to write off bad loans. With individuals, that's almost never the case. Most of us lend money with the expectation (realistic or not) that we'll get it back. As an individual, if you make a loan to your ne'er-do-well brother-in-law—the one with the reputation for blowing his money on booze or bad business ventures—chances are you won't see that money again. You don't have the kind of financial wherewithal a bank has to constantly make bad loans. Yet, individual borrowers who do actually lend money (often to family and friends) make this mistake time and time again.

In addition to reducing their risk by saying no to undesirable would-be borrowers, banking institutions and credit card issuers also have the force of law behind them. They have recourse to put a negative mark on your credit file. They can seize collateralized property. They can send your account to a collection agency. They can sometimes garnish your wages if they get a court judgment against you. And, of course, they can and do impose penalties, fees, and additional interest charges for nonpayment of loans.

Fees and Interest Charges Drive Credit Industry's Profits

Among the top 10 credit card issuers in the United States, punitive interest rates—the rates charged to cardholders who miss a payment or otherwise become delinquent—range from 24.65 to 30.74 percent, according to data from the Coalition for Responsible Credit Practices and CardWeb.com. Some penalty interest rates are at 41%. For instance, CompuCredit, an Atlanta-based issuer of Aspire VISA card, charges an interest rate of prime + 36.25 percent with a 41.00 percent minimum, to its most high-risk cardholders who become delinquent. Translation: borrowers are doling out lots of money to their creditors, while lenders are filling their coffers with more interest and fee income than ever. According to Robert Manning, author of *Credit Card Nation*, bank credit card interest and fee income stood at a combined $28.6 billion in 1990. Today, consumers pay in excess of $64 billion in interest alone, with the average U.S. household forking over about $1,100 in interest to creditors each year. Banks rake in another $30 billion in fee income.

As with escalating interest rates charged, banks are getting richer and richer off of rising fees, not to mention more creative about what types of fees they assess. Besides the dreaded late fees, there are annual fees to contend with, fees for balance transfers, over-the-limit fees, cash-advance fees, foreign currency transaction fees, fees to pay your bill by phone, even fees for account inactivity. What's more, credit card companies in 26 states have no limit on what interest rates they can charge, according to the American Bankers Association. Also, credit card issuers in 27 states can charge whatever the market will bear in terms of annual fees. And as a consumer, your chances of being hit with a fee of some sort—especially a late fee—are greater than ever.

The Good Old Days Are Gone

Remember the good old days when you had a full month to send in your credit card payments? Well, most credit card issuers have shrunk the payment grace period from 30 days to anywhere from 20 to 25 days. If you're late by a day—or even by an hour—you can expect to get hit with a late fee of anywhere from $15 to $40. How can you be late by an hour? Most credit card companies require your payment to be received by an exact hour (sometimes in the morning) in order to be deemed on time. So if the due date is the twelfth of the month, and the company says the payment must be in by 11 a.m., but the postal carrier doesn't deliver the mail with your payment in it until noon, then you're going to get hit with a late fee.

Even more appalling, consumer experts say that if you fail to return your payment in certain creditors' preprinted return envelopes, some card-member agreements give the credit card issuer the right to record receipt of your payment five days after it actually arrives. Under these circumstances, if you've timed your payment to arrive at

> **The lender is always flush with cash, and the borrower is always broke and in debt.**

the creditor's facility on the due date, or even a day or two before it's due, but you use your own envelope, you'll get charged with a late payment. Simply put, the lender is always flush with cash, and the borrower is always broke and in debt. Which would you rather be? It's an easy choice, right? So let's start talking about the pathway to being debt free and how you're going to get there. You must stop borrowing and get out of debt as a vital step in your quest to be a millionaire.

Climbing Out of the Debt Hole

Many of you have read my previous book, *Zero Debt: The Ultimate Guide to Financial Freedom.* It was a *New York Times* bestseller because, among other things, it tapped a nerve among readers nationwide who were struggling with overwhelming debt. In *Zero Debt*, I wrote about how I became debt-free after being mired in $100,000 worth of credit card bills. That's right, $100,000 in credit card debt alone! Fortunately, I was able to pay it all off in three years, without filing for bankruptcy protection, getting credit counseling, or entering a debt management program. To escape the quicksand of debt, I changed my spending patterns and financial habits, and I got smart about my use of credit and credit cards. Believe me, once you get out of debt, you never want to go back into that dark hole again. But if you're not careful, that very thing can happen.

Are You Really Serious about Having Zero Debt?

You can't achieve zero debt until you get serious about not being a borrower anymore. I get e-mails and listen all the time to people who claim to be serious about eliminating their debt, but who aren't will-ing to take the necessary steps to wipe out their debt. There are three clear-cut signs that can tell you whether or not you're serious about being debt-free—or whether you're just kidding yourself. Before I tell you what those three signs are, however, I want you to think for a moment about what it means to be serious about reaching a goal, and what it takes to get there.

Have you ever heard the expression a "serious competitor" or a "serious athlete" as opposed to a recreational or casual athlete? What do you think separates the serious athlete from the casual one? It's that the serious athlete spends enormous amounts of time training, getting in shape, and practicing his or her chosen sport. The serious athlete also actively works at improving his or her game. World class golfer Tiger Woods didn't slack off after winning his first Masters tournament. He still thought he could improve his swing—and he took steps to do so. Serious athletes are also highly consistent in their efforts. They practice discipline daily—whether that means hitting the gym each morning, swimming laps in a pool, or running up and down a ball field to get the exercise they need.

So let's evaluate your behavior. Whereas the serious athlete wants to win a game or be the best competitor in a given sport, your goal is to win in the world of personal finances. Your desire is to get out of debt and achieve financial freedom. In pursuit of that quest, do you devote time to handling your personal finances? Notice that I said "devote" time. Not "steal" time. Not "squeeze in" time. Not even "make time." Nothing short of devotion will do. A person devoted to a cause pays careful, painstaking attention to it.

Many of you might think you spend a lot of time *handling* money issues, but you're really just wasting time by *fretting* over your situation. Unfortunately, however, the time you spend stressing about bills, complaining about not having enough cash for the month, and so forth doesn't count as time devoted toward improving or paying attention to your finances. The main reason is that the time you're putting in is nonproductive time, which just drags you down emotionally and does absolutely nothing concrete to better your financial circumstances.

I'm not asking you to make looking after your finances a second job. But there are 24 hours in a day, or 168 hours in a week. And, yes,

I know you need to sleep. But can you commit to one or two hours a week to shoring up your finances? What will you do during this time? Here's where the second litmus test comes in as far as determining if you're serious about getting out of debt. Your time will be spent proactively working at improving your situation. Some examples might be reading books about personal finances, taking classes or workshops to improve your knowledge in this area, negotiating with creditors, researching potential investments, or finding creative solutions to financial problems—anything that gives you a tangible benefit or helps you control your money, so it's not controlling you.

Finally, are you consistent in doing what it takes to become debt-free? Or are you a cheat? I know that's a strong word. But when you slack off from your financial goals and objectives—say by going on a shopping binge each month—you're really just cheating yourself. I'm not saying that a slipup every now and then means the end of the world. But, if you're seriously determined to get out of debt, you have to evaluate your normal habits and patterns. People who spend a lot of time proactively working on their finances, especially millionaires, don't make a practice out of doing things that undermine those efforts. And neither should you.

Prove Yourself To Yourself

To prove that you're serious about getting out of debt, right now pick a day and time—a minimum of one hour a week—to devote to your finances. Plan to use one of three methods:

1. Spend one straight hour on money matters.

2. Set aside two 30-minute periods of time to handle personal finance issues.

3. Set aside three chunks of 20 minutes for this task.

Decide right now what day you'll do it. Some suggestions: Spend 20 minutes in the morning, 20 minutes on your lunch break, and 20 minutes in the evening one day a week, such as Wednesday. Or pick a day over the weekend, like Saturday, when you can devote an entire hour, uninterrupted, to the task.

Doing this will put you on the road to being debt-free and becoming a millionaire. But you're not done proving yourself—or shall I say proving *to* yourself that you're serious about bettering your financial world. Now make a list of three money matters in your life that you want to get proactive about and immediately address. It may be that you need to pull your credit report and FICO score, enroll in a personal finances course, or make an appointment with a financial planner. Whatever it is, go ahead and do all three things—or at least start the process for whatever needs to be done—this very day.

Last, I want you to get real with yourself. Where have you been cheating? Write down three areas where you've failed to be consistent or where you know you're been erring in handling your finances. It might be the case that you've constantly dipped into your savings or retirement funds without good cause; or perhaps you've allowed your significant other to handle all the household finances because it was too complicated or you were too busy. Whatever the case, I want you to write down the opposite scenario. Describe how you're going to turn that around and become consistent in repairing the broken areas of your financial world. When you've done all three things, you'll know that you're serious.

Get Out of Denial about Your Finances

For those of you making pretty good money, if there's one big obstacle to getting out of debt, it's denying that you have a debt problem. I know, because I was in denial for years about my own situation when

I had $100,000 in credit card debt. Part of my denial stemmed from the fact that I was a high-wage earner, taking home a six-figure salary. But mostly, I was in denial because I was making my payments on time (minimum payments, albeit), and I was doing a lot of other things right with my personal finances, such as insuring myself and regularly investing. Because I was staying afloat and bill collectors weren't calling my house, the subconscious message I was sending myself was: there's nothing wrong with having all these bills as long as I can afford them.

The truth of the matter is that I was kidding myself. I couldn't afford the lifestyle I was living—at least not on a cash basis. In fact, I experienced some of the classic signs and symptoms of a person buried too deep in debt. For instance, I maxed out several credit cards, had a high debt-to-income ratio, and I often used credit as a substitute for cash—allowing me to make big-ticket purchases on the spot whether I could afford them or not. I also constantly switched credit cards in order to take advantage of the lowest possible interest rates, thereby keeping my payments relatively low. While this can be a smart strategy to decrease finance charges, it's indicative of a larger problem when you find that you *need* to keep transferring balances just to be able to swing the minimum payments due. Additionally, I had way too many credit cards—more than a dozen at one point. Some other telltale signs that you have excessive debts are:

- You skip payments you can't afford.
- You argue a lot with your partner about bills.
- You lose sleep or feel stressed out over your debts.
- You get turned down when you apply for new credit.
- You receive phone calls from creditors or bill collectors.
- You use credit for everyday purchases like gas or groceries.
- You have a low FICO credit score because of the debts you carry.

If any of these symptoms describe you, trust me, you are likely operating in a danger zone with your credit cards and your debts—even if you don't yet realize it.

Put Everything You Owe in Writing

To start knocking off your debts, create a written list or a spreadsheet itemizing each creditor and the full amount owed. For some people, this step will be a big eye-opener. You may find out that your debts have snuck up on you and you now have far more debt than you thought. For others, putting all your obligations in black and white may give you some comfort if you discover that your situation isn't as dire as you'd anticipated. However things turn out, it pays to have your bills listed in writing so you can start your plan of attack.

Once you itemize your debts, pull your credit card statements and write down the name of your creditors, their addresses, the total amount you owe, the minimum payment due, and the interest rate you're being charged. To make sure you haven't forgotten any creditors, now is the time to order your credit reports from http://www.myfico.com. If you go online to that Fair Isaac Web site, you'll be able to get your FICO credit scores and credit reports instantly online from all three credit bureaus—Equifax, Experian and TransUnion. Those reports should list all the credit accounts you have outstanding. The point is that you want to know exactly how much you owe for all your consumer debts. And you don't want to guesstimate. So if you know you've charged on your cards since receiving the last statement, then you should call the customer service number on the card and listen to your most recent, up-to-date balance and minimum payment due. Besides helping you to track your debts, having a list of your creditors is also helpful if your wallet or purse gets stolen or your credit cards somehow get lost.

> **You need a clear picture of your finances in order to move forward in your quest to become a millionaire.**

While you may find the prospect of tallying up all your bills daunting, writing down all your bills will actually provide you with some relief because part of the anxiety many people experience over their credit card debts and other bills is to the result of uncertainty. Uncertainty about how much is really owed collectively; uncertainty about how the bills will get paid; or uncertainty about where all the money is going each month. You really need a clear picture of your finances in order to move forward in your quest to become a millionaire. Therefore, you can't afford to "have a rough idea" about debts. Do you owe $3,900 or is it more like $9,300 or more?

Getting your bills listed in black and white is a surefire way to start simplifying your finances and seeing where your cash is going. To get a jumpstart on this process, go to the Free Info area of my Web site at http://www.themoneycoach.net and download the form called "I Debticate Myself to Being Debt Free." This is a spreadsheet you can print out for your own private use. Enter all the information I've suggested above concerning your credit accounts.

Don't Spend What You Don't Have

The average U.S. household spends $1.22 for every $1.00 it earns, according to a survey by Northwestern Mutual. That's a sure way to stay in debt forever. Sometimes people get so depressed about their debts that they actually go out shopping—and become even deeper in debt. Don't fall into that trap. It will only exacerbate your financial difficulties. Also, if you're in debt and you're serious about trying to get out, then it's imperative that you not make any additional purchases with credit that you can't immediately pay off. So just realize that, if you engage in any future shopping and spending that you finance over time, what you're really doing is continuing the habits of a borrower, making your credit card lenders richer, and sinking further into the quicksand of debt.

Use Cash More Often

Studies show that people spend more, or overspend, when they buy goods and services with credit rather than paying for these items with cold hard cash. Think about it: you're more apt to really consider the wisdom of a $100 purchase when you have to fork over that hard-earned hundred dollar bill—as opposed to whipping out a credit card that allows you to think, "I'll just pay for this later." I'm not suggesting that you cut up your credit cards. Or that you stop using credit altogether. I don't think either of those strategies is effective, in the long run, in terms of helping you to become a financially responsible, creditworthy consumer. What I am recommending, however, is that you become more conscious about your everyday purchases and that you get out of the habit of automatically paying for things with credit cards.

Cut Spending and Apply Savings To Debt

As a consumer, you should always be on the lookout for easy ways to slash your spending. Whether you're doing grocery shopping, getting your clothes dry-cleaned, or purchasing a new laptop, it's not wise to pay a penny more than necessary, especially when higher prices don't always translate into better quality. I don't think you should sacrifice in areas that are important to you and that hold value for you. Remember when you created your Personal Prosperity Plan and you itemized a variety of things in your Millionaire-in-Training Budget? Well, as you start cutting back on unnecessary spending, don't make your cuts so deep that you don't enjoy spending on the things you want. If you do, it will only cause you to go off track and not stick to your budget. But I will say that you should consider this area a unique challenge. Get creative about your finances. Look at ways in which you can clearly save money by shopping around or by modifying some of your spending habits. Come up with a list of at least five things you can do to curb your spending.

Once you get going, many of you will come up with far more than five areas. Also think about major categories of spending where you can reduce your costs. For those of you who pay a monthly car note, consider refinancing your auto loan in order to save yourself money. Go to http://www.capitaloneauto.com, the country's largest online auto lender, to save money on your monthly vehicle payments. I also recommend you visit another great financial Web site, http://www. lowermybills.com. This is a tremendous site for anyone seeking to save money in a variety of areas ranging from home equity loans to auto insurance to long-distance telephone service. Best of all, it's a free service that does comparison shopping for you in 18 categories of household bills. Whatever cost savings you achieve—from clipping coupons to canceling unnecessary magazine subscriptions—make sure you apply that extra money to your debts.

Pay at Least Twice the Minimum Due

Starting in 2006, a federal law requires credit card companies to impose minimum payments that cover at least some of your principal balance, along with interest and fees charged. The good news is that this law will force consumers to wipe out their debts sooner rather than later. The bad news is that cash-strapped households have higher monthly payments to handle. In the past credit card companies typically asked you to pay 2 percent of your outstanding balance. But to comply with the law, credit card companies are now asking that you pay roughly 4 percent of your outstanding balance. Even with these higher minimum requirements, you have to realize that if you make only the bare minimum payments on cards with big balances, you'll still stay mired in debt for years.

For example, let's say that you carry a $10,000 balance on a card with a 16 percent interest rate. If you make a 2 percent minimum monthly payment, it will take you more than 40 years to pay off the debt, and it will cost you an

> **Pay at least two times the minimum amount due, and three times the amount if possible.**

additional $19,329 in interest. With a 4 percent minimum payment, your debt will be repaid in roughly 14 years, and you'll shell out an extra $4,931 in interest costs, according to Howard Dvorkin, founder of the nonprofit Consolidated Credit Counseling Services, Inc., and author of *Credit Hell: How to Dig Out of Debt*. In an ideal world, you'd pay off your balances in full each month. But obviously that's not feasible for everyone. So strive to pay at least two times the minimum amount due, and three times is even more desirable. That's what I did when I got serious about knocking out my $100,000 in credit card debts. Tripling up on those minimum payments also felt good psychologically, as I watched my balances decline over time. When you need motivation to keep doling out all that money to the credit card companies, just remember that minimum payments are a pitfall that only lifelong borrowers fall victim to, because "minimum" payments in the short run really mean "maximum" payments in the long run.

Pay Your Bills Ahead of the Due Dates

We've already discussed how banks are shortening the grace periods on credit cards, so it should be obvious that you need to get your monthly payments in on time. But you should go one step further. Don't stress yourself by trying to time your payments to arrive on the creditor's doorstep precisely on the due date. There's too much risk of something going wrong. A better strategy is to plan to pay your bills well ahead of their due dates. For most people, getting your payments in a week before they're due is sufficient. This way, you stay ahead of your debts by making sure you don't inadvertently send in a payment late and get hit with a late fee. In general, when it comes to handling your personal finances—as well as other areas of your life—you'll find it so much more peaceful and efficient if you make a habit out of doing things early rather than at the last minute.

Cut Money-Draining Relatives and Friends Out of Your (Financial) Life

I may take a lot of heat for saying this, but sometimes getting rid of your debts and building the wealth you desire is largely a matter of getting rid of certain people in your life—at least your financial life. You'll recall that I tell you in Chapter 2 to learn to give to others and that you would be blessed for it. I stand by that statement. It's also true, however, that if you're going to become a millionaire, you'll have to learn to say no when necessary. No to grown, able-bodied freeloaders who try to take advantage of you or make you feel guilty for not helping them because, allegedly, you have money to spare. No to schemers who concoct one cockamamie business idea after another and expect you to continually invest good money after bad in their failed efforts. No to dreamers who have big plans to go back to school, start a business, or fulfill some other lifelong dream (with your money, of course), but then never follow through on these plans. No to individuals who sport new clothes and jewelry every time you see them, but for some reason can't seem to pay their car note, rent, or gas bill on time, and then expect you to bail them out of one crisis after another. No to people who think, in short, that you are their very own personal ATM, bank teller, savings account, and rainy-day fund all rolled up into one.

And as harsh as it may seem, you need to establish boundaries when it comes to finances, friends, and family. Too often, would-be millionaires get dragged down by those closest to them who may not have their financial acts together. It's one thing to help someone out of a jam, or to be outright generous from the kindness of your heart because you want to express support to someone. But it's another matter entirely to be called upon time and time again to take financial responsibility for adults who, by rights, should be held accountable for managing their own financial affairs. If you have people in your life who rely on you as their financial backup plan, you are doing yourself and them a huge disservice.

To break this cycle, have a one-on-one conversation with anyone you deem necessary, in which you explain that your days of serving as a piggy bank are over. Needless to say, you don't have to be that blunt about it. But you should be direct enough to tell that person something like this:

Ensuring your own financial stability first and foremost is a difficult but necessary part of being a millionaire.

> I want to talk to you about finances. I've started doing a lot more financial planning and looking at areas where I'm spending money in my personal life. In the past, you've come to me on a number of occasions for money, and I've given it to you, thinking I was helping. I don't feel comfortable doing that anymore. I now see that when I repeatedly give you money, it sends the wrong message—and suggests that you don't always have to be financially responsible for yourself. The truth of the matter is that you do. I want you to learn proper money management skills and to watch your spending so that you don't have to rely on me for money. I want to maintain a close relationship with you, but I also want to establish some boundaries when it comes to money. So please don't ask for

me to pay your bills or provide you with loans in the future. I hope you understand that I still value you, and I'm not trying to hurt your feelings or offend you. But I need to tell you this for your own good, as well as for my own peace of mind.

Obviously, this is just a sample script. Say whatever comes naturally and whatever is necessary and appropriate for your circumstances. Expect to have to reiterate your message a few times for it to really sink in. And anticipate that you'll probably have to reinforce this message at the most inopportune time—like when the individual in question is asking you for money yet again. If you don't stick to your guns, he or she won't think you are serious and the money-draining cycle will continue in perpetuity.

Ensuring your own financial stability first and foremost is a difficult but necessary part of being a millionaire. It's kind of like being on an airplane when the stewardess is giving the passengers the safety instructions. They always say that in the event of an emergency you should put your own oxygen mask on first, and then offer assistance to children or others who may require help. The theory behind this practice is: What good will you be to those around you if you lose consciousness or become mentally unstable at high altitudes? So it is with your finances. You have to safeguard your money, even if you have a lot of it, in order to maintain financial stability and to be around to help out when you are truly needed.

Evaluate the People, Places, and Products that Cause You To Spend Money

While you're extricating yourself from those who may be a financial drain, you also need to consider a related aspect of your spending that may be driving you into debt. In particular, you need to take a long hard look at the people, places, and products that cause you to spend your hard-earned dollars. For example, do you notice that, whenever you go out with your office mate on a lunch break, the two of you invariably wind up at the mall—picking up perfume or a pair of shoes in the process? And what about being online? Is that a place that seems to bring out the shopping gene in you? If that's the case, you may need to curb you Internet surfing activities until you can stay away from all those pop-up advertisements enticing you to spend money.

Then, too, there may be certain products that you fall for hook, line, and sinker—whether or not you want or need them. Whatever "it" is, we all have products that we just "have to have." If you're not careful, hanging out with a shopping buddy, going to places where you know you'll be tempted to spend recklessly, or constantly allowing to-die-for items to dangle before your eyes can drive you deeper into debt.

Build Up a Cash Cushion

Ideally, you should have three months' expenses set aside for emergencies (the six Dreaded Ds), like downsizing, disability, or divorce. That means if your bills are $3,000 a month, you should have a $9,000 cash cushion. Most people find it difficult to build up a savings account worth three months of their expenses. The trick is to amass the funds little by little. Just start putting aside whatever you can afford now, and do it on a consistent basis. Consider that money to be untouchable in terms of financing your everyday purchases or your normal monthly expenditures. Your cash savings are to protect you when unexpected things occur. Without these savings as your safety net, you'll always be forced to pay for

Set three months' expenses aside for emergencies.

emergencies with credit, you'll always be a borrower, and you'll never achieve zero debt.

Get Financial Help

Millionaires know the value of having qualified financial experts on their side. In fact, it's not uncommon for millionaires to have a team of advisers who specialize in a variety of personal finance areas, everything from taxes to retirement planning. Even though you may not yet be a millionaire, don't think for a minute that hiring financial help is only for people who have "already arrived," financially speaking.

Retaining the advice of a financial expert also doesn't have to be that expensive. Go to the Financial Planning Association (FPA) for a certified financial planner in your neighborhood. The FPA can be reached toll-free at (800) 647-6340 or on the Internet at http://www.fpanet.org. The National Association of Personal Financial Advisors (NAPFA) is also another great place to find qualified fee-only advisers who don't work on commission. You can contact NAPFA at (800) 366-2732 or online at http://www.napfa.org. I also teach personal finance workshops and seminars, and I run financial boot camps where you can receive online and group tele-coaching from anywhere in the country, as well as individualized coaching to help you reach your financial goals. You can learn more about my personal finance education initiatives by visiting http://www.themoneycoach.net.

Use Windfalls Properly

Some people struggling to get out of debt and get past the drudgery of being a borrower are fortunate enough to come into cash windfalls that could be used to pay off outstanding debt. This windfall might be a tax refund check, an inheritance, proceeds from a lawsuit, an insurance payout, money from a legal settlement, an annual bonus—anything that represents a lump sum of money beyond your regular paycheck or your normal income. Unfortunately, too many people waste lump sums of money on spending sprees of all kinds.

If you should receive any large chunk of money, particularly an unexpected cash windfall, there's probably no better use for those funds than eliminating your credit card debt. Don't blow a great opportunity to put yourself in the black by wiping out those pernicious consumer debts if you are the recipient of any kind of windfall.

What's Your Money Personality?

We've all heard the saying that opposites attract. Nowhere is this saying truer than when it comes to dealing with money. All across the country, millions of couples have financial battles each day, largely because their money personalities clash and they haven't figured out how to overcome those differences. Well, just as men and women often appear to be speaking two different languages, so it is that the couples involved in personal relationships often can't understand why the other party seems to be so irrational in handling financial matters. And even more battles rage internally between what you know you should be doing to manage your money wisely and your money personality demons. Can these opposing viewpoints ever peacefully coexist? The answer is yes. It's not always easy, but, whether the conflict is internal or between partners, it is possible for drastically different money perspectives to achieve harmony. But first you have to understand what money personality type best describes you. I've created a brief quiz to give you a quick snapshot of yourself and hopefully let you see some aspects of your financial personality a lot more clearly.

WHAT IS YOUR MONEY PERSONALITY?

1. If my car breaks down, the roof leaks, or some other emergency arises, then:

A. I don't think it would be a problem, because I try to put aside money for emergencies.

B. I would be financially stressed—yet again. My money is so tight that even though I want to put aside a little extra savings, so far I haven't been able to do so.

C. I'd use the savings from my emergency fund that I've built up over time. Hopefully, it would be enough to cover any situation.

D. I would just use my credit cards to pay for it, and figure out how to pay them off later.

E. I probably wouldn't panic since I tend to budget for those kinds of things.

F. I would be in a financial bind. But I think things would eventually work out somehow.

2. Right now, my retirement savings account:

A. Is growing slowly but surely.

B. What retirement savings account? I can barely pay the bills I have today.

C. Is fairly well funded. But I still worry about outliving my money.

D. Is next to nothing. I've put aside only a little bit for retirement, or I've had to borrow from my retirement account to make ends meet.

E. Is right about where it should be. I'm on target to reach my retirement savings goals.

F. Isn't on my mind right now. Since retirement is in the future, I figure why worry about that today?

3. **If somebody gave me $25,000 unexpectedly, my first thought would be:**

A. Great. I'll be able to add a chunk of this money to my savings account.

B. Now I can buy something I've wanted to get for myself, a family member, or friend.

C. I'll put this money away for a rainy day. I might need it in the future.

D. Yes!!!!!!!! Now who can I get to hit the mall with me?

E. How can I invest this money wisely?

F. What charities can I donate this to in order to change the world?

4. **When it comes to credit card bills:**

A. I almost always pay off the entire balance due each month.

B. I often pay the minimum amount due, or I have missed a payment recently.

C. I have little or no debt because I rarely use credit.

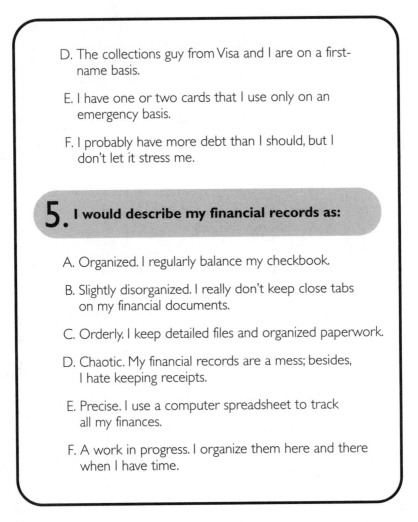

D. The collections guy from Visa and I are on a first-name basis.

E. I have one or two cards that I use only on an emergency basis.

F. I probably have more debt than I should, but I don't let it stress me.

5. I would describe my financial records as:

A. Organized. I regularly balance my checkbook.

B. Slightly disorganized. I really don't keep close tabs on my financial documents.

C. Orderly. I keep detailed files and organized paperwork.

D. Chaotic. My financial records are a mess; besides, I hate keeping receipts.

E. Precise. I use a computer spreadsheet to track all my finances.

F. A work in progress. I organize them here and there when I have time.

Now review your answers to see the letters you checked most: Were they primarily As, Bs, Cs, Ds, Es, or Fs? It's also possible that you're a "hybrid," with leanings toward *more than one type* of personality. But for the most part, you probably have certain dominant traits when it comes to your money personality. Keep on reading for a description of the following money personality types: saver, spender, stasher, splurger, goal-setter, or dreamer.

Your Money Personality Type
REVEALED!

If your answers fall mostly under one letter, then your money personality type is revealed:

Mostly As: **Saver**—You are a saver if you regularly set aside money and make a point of building a cash cushion for a rainy day.

Mostly Bs: **Spender**—You are a spender if you pretty much spend everything you earn (and possibly *more* than you earn); are living paycheck to paycheck; or often buy frivolous or luxury items that you can't afford.

Mostly Cs: **Stasher**—You are a stasher if you are an extreme form of a saver; you worry excessively (or unnecessarily) about having money in the future, so you hoard it now, often to the point where you do not enjoy your money or the things money can buy.

Mostly Ds: **Splurger**—You are a splurger if you are an extreme version of a spender; you may or may not spend everything you make, but you frequently succumb to impulse purchases, buy large-ticket items, or buy spontaneously and often later regret it.

Mostly Es: **Goal-Setter**—You are a goal-setter if you prefer to spend your money on items or activities that are budgeted, carefully calculated, and/or planned in advance.

Mostly Fs: **Dreamer**—You are a dreamer if you have a lot of big dreams for material success but no practical financial plans about how to reach your goals.

In my experience, those with saver and goal-setter money personalities are usually those who can most readily become millionaires. However, that's not to suggest that spenders and even splurgers can't achieve millionaire status, so long as they're willing to modify certain behaviors and keep in check the "bad" parts of their money personalities.

Couples and Money

For couples dealing with financial battles, the first step toward resolving conflict is to share what lessons you learned as a child about money. Remember in Chapter 1 when I asked you to reflect on the overt and subtle messages that parents and other adults taught you? Well, now's the time to clue your partner in on these things. You may think he's being stingy with money, when in reality he's simply responding to the fears and anxieties he experienced growing up in a household where money was scarce. Or perhaps you have a conversation with your partner about why she likes to spend recklessly (at least in your eyes) or handle money in a way that you don't approve, and you discover that because your significant other lost a parent early in life, that loss caused the person to adopt a carefree "you can't take it with you" attitude about material things.

Whatever the case, communication is crucial. If you discover, as will likely be the case, that you and your honey have money personalities that are polar opposites, don't fret. It doesn't mean the relationship is doomed. Nor does it foretell a lifetime of knock-down, drag out battles over the family budget. What it does require, however, is that you both establish a mutually agreed upon set of boundaries in which you can live peacefully. For instance, the saver striving to boost the family's financial security should be allowed to consistently sock away a reasonable amount of money each month—without being called a tightwad or feeling guilty about his or her need to save. By the same token, the spender should not be put on such a tight leash that he or she feels browbeaten about making the smallest of purchases. Rather, the spender should agree to a fixed amount of money that can be spent in a given month, an amount that won't break the family's bank, drive the couple into debt, or sacrifice its financial well-being.

YOURS, MINE AND OURS

From a practical, financial, and emotional standpoint, it can also make sense to establish "his" and "her" bank accounts. Some people frown upon the notion of separate accounts. They say anything other than joint accounts creates a "me" situation versus an "us" mentality. Critics also think "his" and "her" accounts reduce marriage to a business arrangement. Nevertheless, I truly believe that separate accounts can be very healthy for couples, when done properly. For example, you might have a joint account from which you pay household bills, and then separate accounts from which each party can make discretionary purchases of his or her own choosing. This way, neither person in the relationship has to ask the other individual for "permission" to spend on this or that.

The advantages of having individual accounts are many. Some separation of money can be fine for couples in order for them to decrease squabbles when there are different money styles or varying views about money's purpose, as is the case when one party values money for the power, status, or control it can bring, while the other half of the couple subscribes to the notion that money is to be used for, say, fun, entertainment, or stability. Separate accounts also foster economic independence and confidence, especially for women. And having your own financial accounts also helps each party develop money management and budgeting skills. Finally, having individual accounts can actually help keep a relationship fresh and fun-loving. When you have your own money, you have the ability to take your partner out on a date, buy him or her an unexpected gift from time to time, or foot the bill for a romantic weekend trip—without the other person worrying about "How much is this costing us?" Ultimately, all these things bring about greater financial and marital harmony.

DON'T TOLERATE FINANCIAL ABUSE

Certainly, though, there is the possibility of one party in a relationship abusing the separate accounts concept. I've heard, for instance, of people who have discovered that their spouse was hiding money or secretly stashing away assets. Most often, the parties in the dark were women. But certainly, men are sometimes unaware of funds their wives may be squirreling away. If you should find yourself in such a situation, my advice is to be direct with your partner, but not confrontational. Start by simply asking: "Why?" If the person wanted a separate account for the sake of independence or to save for a certain goal, then it's probably not worth making a federal case out of the matter. You should just express your feelings about discovering the "hidden" money, and encourage your partner to better communicate with you in the future. But just because you're in love doesn't mean that you should be blinded by that love. Don't easily dismiss major red flags about your joint finances and warning signs that your partner may be building a financial fortress that doesn't include you. Some examples of these red flags include:

- You're inexplicably off the mortgage.
- You're suddenly off the car ownership papers.
- You're no longer the 401(k) beneficiary.
- You're been removed as the primary life insurance beneficiary.
- Your partner has taken equity out of the house, cashed out assets acquired jointly or made big financial transactions without your knowledge or consent.

In these instances, you should first do a bit of independent investigating on your own to find out what happened. Then begin to have some serious, detailed conversations with your partner about what transpired, when and why. You should also seek to have the situation reversed if you feel you are being financially disenfranchised. Unfortunately, when some people are plotting divorce, they may secretly take some of the steps mentioned above, before announcing their desires for divorce to their partners. You don't want to be caught completely unaware in such a scenario. So if any red-flag situation does occur or if you find out about a very large separate account that you had no clue about, you should also inquire about other "secret" accounts.

Just because you discovered one account doesn't mean there aren't others, or other assets—such as real estate holdings—that you may not have been told about. Do what's necessary at that point to protect your financial interests. While I do advocate separate accounts, I don't think it's healthy for the relationship to be deceitful about their existence. Besides, if you're in a committed relationship—particularly one that you hope will last a lifetime—the more you can do as a couple to reach your goals and improve your finances, the sooner you'll both reach millionaire status. After all, what good is it to have a ton of money if you don't have anyone you love to share it with?

Once you and your mate reduce or eliminate your high-interest rate credit card debt, and start putting money aside to build up that all-important cash cushion, now you're ready to begin investing. Next, I tell you how to take the money you had been throwing out the window on credit card payments, and put those funds to work in ways that can quickly help you become a millionaire.

4

LEVERAGE THE POWER
OF PROPERTY

If it's true that money talks, then leverage is truly the language of
millionaires. *Leverage,* simply put, is the ability to spend the least
amount of a given resource—whether it's time, money, effort, or
something else—and get maximum results. Wealthy people know the
power of using leverage all too well. In fact, the proper use of leverage
in acquiring real estate has made many a person very, very rich. Experts
say that more than 90 percent of all millionaires own real estate, either
their own primary residence or investment property. Very often,
millionaires own both—adding considerably to their net worth.

In this chapter, I let you in on smart ways you can acquire real estate,
whether you're trying to come up with the down payment to buy your
first home or are seeking creative ways to add to your existing portfolio
of property holdings. I also tell you why real estate frequently outperforms every other investment you might consider. I explain to you
the tremendous benefits of owning property—as well as the drawbacks
and myths associated with investing in real estate. By the time we're
done, you will have calculated your own net worth, as well as learned

> **Leverage is the language of millionaires.**

how to implement a number of real estate investing strategies that can help you join the millionaires club.

The Case for Buying Real Estate Now—and Always

I have to admit that of the range of investments one can possibly choose from—everything from gold or other commodities to paper assets like stocks and bonds to nontraditional assets such as art or collectibles—real estate is my absolute favorite. It represents something tangible you can see and touch. It's not complicated to understand. Real estate offers numerous financial benefits. And it's also the most fun. I just love looking at homes, whether they're old or new, and envisioning the various ways I could make them better—and make a buck in the process.

But I'm not here to tell you how to have fun with your finances. I'm here to tell you how to accumulate wealth and keep it. If that's your goal, then real estate definitely deserves to be a significant part of your asset base for many reasons. For starters, because it is not correlated to the stock or bond markets, real estate can diversify your investment portfolio. Real estate can also act as a hedge against inflation. It offers

> **Real estate provides you with the chance to use leverage to dramatically add to your net worth in ways that no other investment can match.**

significant tax benefits: in addition to depreciation write-offs, in most cases, the sale of investment property held for at least a year is taxed at capital gains rates—15 percent for most people, which is far below the top income tax rate of 35 percent.

Owning property gives you the chance to capture price appreciation in the market, something that—while not guaranteed—certainly happens far more often than not. Additionally, real estate can generate significant cash flow—often far more than stocks. For instance, the average company in the Standard & Poor's 500 Stock Index has an annual dividend yield of 1.1 percent, compared with a 7 percent average yield for real estate. The cash flow from real estate comes from rental income. Your tenants basically pay your monthly mortgage—and hopefully provide you with additional profit—while your property increases in value and your mortgage balance decreases. As a property owner, you also build equity with every mortgage payment that's made. You can tap this equity whenever you need money to do anything from financing an addition to your home to paying for your child's education. If you ask me, all these benefits mean that real estate is always in vogue.

The Power of Leverage

Best of all, real estate provides you with the chance to use leverage to dramatically add to your net worth in ways that no other investment can match. To illustrate the phenomenal power of leverage, assume that you have $10,000 to invest any way you like. You could choose to buy pork bellies, shares in a Fortune 500 company, high-yielding corporate bonds, or something else. Now let's say your investment rises 10 percent over the course of a year. That means you've added $1,000 to your initial $10,000 investment. So your investment is now worth $11,000. Your return, in dollar terms, is $1,000. But what if you took that same initial investment of $10,000 and decided to use it as a 10 percent down payment on a house that cost $100,000. For the sake of comparing apples to apples, let's say that this property also goes up by 10 percent after one year. Now that house is worth $110,000. This means that your $10,000 investment also earned you a $10,000 gain—or a 100 percent return on your money.

And that return doesn't even take into account the other aforementioned advantages of owning real estate. You can see how real estate lets you purchase a big asset with a relatively small amount of money and make optimal use of your own funds—no matter how limited they may be. This is leverage at its best. When you leverage the power of property, you dramatically increase your asset base, help develop a rock-solid financial foundation that could last for generations, and boost your net worth all at the same time.

Better Than the Stock Market—Most of the Time

From a pure numbers standpoint, the best investment I've ever made was buying a piece of land in 2001 for $37,500 and selling it in 2004 for $200,000. That's an incredible 433 percent return—far better than most stock market gains. No wonder I love real estate, right? Well, actually there have been instances when I've never wanted to see another shred of investment property. Like the time I bought a three-family home with the intention of renovating it and flipping it for a quick, fat profit. What a nightmare that turned out to be.

First, the property wound up being in far worse shape than it initially appeared. Instead of just paint, carpet, and updated appliances, this place needed a complete overhaul: new roof, 56 new windows, new kitchens and bathrooms, upgraded wiring—even new copper plumbing after some desperate criminal stole the first set of plumbing I had installed. Then there were the headaches with the contractor and his subcontractors: shoddy work, constant and unexplained work delays; and costs that rose well above the original quotes. What was supposed to be a 60-day project that would yield a cool $50,000 turned instead into a 10-month ordeal that netted just $20,000. Hardly worth all the work, time, effort, and money invested. As these two examples show, you can make big fortunes in real estate or sometimes walk away with next to nothing for your troubles—or even worse, suffer a loss.

Creating My Own "Luck"

With the land deal, I sat on a piece of property and benefited from pure price appreciation. Some might say I got lucky. I say I created my own luck by doing the three most important things that any real estate investor can do: performing adequate due diligence; acting decisively on a deal when opportunity presents itself; and exercising the patience necessary to reap the financial benefits that only accrue over time. Let me tell you what happened in between the time my ex-husband and I bought and sold this land.

For starters, they were actually two pieces of land; each one 25 feet wide, and situated side by side to make up one big plot that was a total of 50 feet by 110 feet. I purchased the land at an auction held by the city of Newark, New Jersey. Would you believe the land was originally listed for less than $3,000? But the bidding got so intense that the price quickly escalated. After being outbid on another property during the auction, I was determined to get this land. I'd done my homework. I'd driven up and down street after street for months on end scouring possible buildings or land to buy. I knew that Newark—though written off by some as a city in urban decay—was really in the early phase of a full-fledged turnaround.

The downtown area was thriving. Major businesses were setting up shop in the city. An impressive effort to upgrade Newark's technology and transportation system was underway. Of course, it also didn't hurt that Newark is a short train ride away from the world's financial capital: New York City. Even more promising, I was sure the land would be worthwhile, because it was in a section of Newark that was clearly on its way back. Development was taking place everywhere nearby. Real estate investors big and small could smell opportunity— and it showed in the tremendous explosion of new multifamily residences and rehabilitated homes in the area. I also knew that these city-owned properties were hard to come by. Yet they represented (potentially, at least) the cheapest way to acquire land in the city. So I decided to go for it and pony up the money necessary—$37,500—to outbid everyone else.

THE REAL WORK BEGINS

Securing the land, however, was far from the end of the deal. The plan was to build a couple of multifamily residences on the land and sell them after one year—in order to take advantage of more favorable long-term capital gains rates. Therefore, a fence had to be erected around the property. The land had to be surveyed and insured. Title insurance was also required. Annual property taxes had to be paid on the land. Clean-up work had to be done several times to remove debris, overgrown grass and bushes, and litter. A sign advertising future homes was put up—and then vandalized, so it had to be removed. While all this ongoing maintenance was taking place, we were in talks with builders, architects, and engineers in a bid to get two new multifamily homes built on the site. Many, many discussions were also held with city officials and others to confirm zoning laws and all manner of ordinances and building regulations.

I remember spending days researching modular home builders online and then ultimately taking a two-hour trip to the facilities of Westchester Modular Home builders in New York to check out their plant and the company's capabilities. Back then, however, I was working full time in corporate America, and my ex-husband was in school full-time pursuing his Ph.D. Since we were also juggling raising two young kids, you can see why we never quite completed building anything at all on the land. We ultimately decided to just sit on it and sell it later.

Then came the slew of offers in late 2003 and early 2004. The real estate market in Newark got even more heated as developers, real estate investors, agents, and others all began calling, writing, and offering to buy that land. When an offer for $120,000 came in, we thought it was good, but not good enough. Pat Massenberg, a friend of mine who also has a real estate license, suggested that I list the property for sale on the Multiple Listing Service (MLS) to see what price the market would bear. Her recommended listing price: $200,000. It didn't take a full week for a buyer to meet our asking price. So, yes, if you call all of that "luck," then I'm a real estate investor of the luckiest sort. I tell you this story, however, to give you a fair and accurate picture of what you can expect as a real estate investor.

Real Estate Myths about Profits, Taxes, and Time

I honestly believe that amazing wealth can be built through real estate. I'm living proof of that. But I'd also be derelict in my duties as your Money Coach if I didn't tell you that—based on my experience as well as the insights of many other real estate experts—you should not think for a minute that real estate is your pathway to overnight riches. In fact, the biggest misconceptions that would-be investors have about real estate involve: (1) the profits they will make; (2) the tax benefits they will reap; and (3) the amount of time they will have to devote to various real estate ventures. Let's look briefly at each one of these. I know that all of you have heard some wild claims about how real estate can make you rich quick, fast, and in a hurry. Peruse your local book store or look online and you'll see many, many books, articles, and Web sites that promise triple-digit real estate returns, with speedy results.

Aside from tempting you with the idea that you can invest in property part time, in your spare time, or on the weekend, these real estate gurus throw out eye-popping profit figures, with lots of zeros at the end. The reality, though, is that for the vast majority of people who have built wealth through real estate, the get-rich-quick methods were not what they used. Instead of flipping properties, they relied on long-term investing strategies, wringing the most possible benefits out of their real estate holdings.

> **I'm living proof that amazing wealth can be built through real estate.**

Tax Breaks and Tax Traps with Real Estate

Whether you're searching for an out-of-state vacation home, looking around locally for a small apartment building to manage, or are thinking about venturing into commercial real estate, there's no question that investing in real estate offers you the chance to gain a regular stream of income and reap the reward of long-term appreciation. But will you enjoy big tax benefits? Sure, there are plenty to be had—with plenty of exceptions as well. That's why the smartest real estate investors know that buying property has its own set of complexities, risks, and realities when it comes to taxes and dealing with Uncle Sam.

How much (or how little) you will pay in taxes and how extensively you can take advantage of an array of tax and financial benefits is guided primarily by whether or not the IRS considers you a "professional" real estate investor. In your mind, you may be saying: "Of course I am!" After all, you know that you put in a great deal of time to acquire and manage properties, not to mention the time spent finding the right tenants, screening would-be renters, collecting rents, and so forth. Still, for all your hard work, the reality is that the IRS may say that you're still not active enough to get all the tax breaks you so often hear about for real estate investors. For starters, the government has very strict rules about who qualifies as a *bona fide* professional real estate investor. According to the Internal Revenue Service, to be a professional, you have to spend more than 750 hours a year in real estate activity. On top of that, more than half of all your working hours must have been spent in the property trade or business. If you don't meet those requirements, right off the bat your real estate dealings will be deemed as a passive investment.

Passive Investors Versus Professional Real Estate Pros

There are very serious—and financially significant—consequences to having the IRS deem you a passive investor. Undoubtedly, you're in this industry to make money. But any real estate veteran will tell you that losses are inevitable, due to costly or unexpected repairs, vacancies that last longer than anticipated, tenants who don't pay, and so on. The IRS says that investors in passive activities are limited in the amount of passive losses they can deduct—meaning you don't immediately get a tax break for these losses. And in some cases, you may not ever get a tax break. Here's why: federal law states that losses incurred by passive real estate investors can be used only to offset gains from other passive activities. And here again, the IRS has hard-and-fast rules about what qualifies as passive activities. For example, partnership income and rental income from real estate count as passive income. But your salary or W-2 wages from a job, any dividends you earn, or investment income are not treated as passive income.

In practical terms, here's how the passive status affects you. If you have losses from real estate and no passive income, more than likely you can't actually utilize those losses (and get a tax break from them) until you actually sell your interest in the real estate. The idea is that, as an investor, you'll make a gain by selling the property for a price higher than what you paid for it. The gain or profit on that sale is considered passive income. The passive losses that have built up over the years can now be used to offset that passive income. Another way to handle this situation, though, is to carry forward passive losses and use them to offset passive income at some future time. This option is certainly better than not being able to claim your losses at all. But it's small consolation for you in the current year when you experience large expenses and suffer a loss on your real estate investment.

> **Investors in passive activities are limited in the amount of passive losses they can deduct.**

What about if you're financing real estate? Once again, you can get a tax break—within limits. For example, you're allowed to deduct mortgage interest, but this deduction is also determined by passive-loss rules. Therefore, there are caps, tied to income and other factors, on how much mortgage interest you can legally write off. I wish there were a one-size-fits all set of guidelines that governed passive losses. Unfortunately, the rules on passive losses, like much of the U.S. tax codes, are complicated and technical. Additionally, state laws can differ from federal law. In New Jersey, for instance, there are no state passive-loss rules. However, real estate investors in New Jersey are still subject to federal passive-loss rules.

Drawbacks to Real Estate

Besides tricky federal or state rules that might limit the tax breaks you can get, there are other drawbacks to investing in property. For starters, real estate investments are far less liquid and typically require a much longer holding period than stocks or bonds. Also, there can be a relatively high cost of entry in real estate deals. In an economic downturn, real estate prices can really take a hit, as happened in the early 1990s.

> **Real estate investments are far less liquid and typically require a much longer holding period than stocks or bonds.**

Also, valuations sometimes can be difficult to establish. How do you know, for example, whether that 10-acre parcel of land in Florida is really worth a mint if there are no bidders? Just because a broker—who wants to earn a commission—says a piece of real estate is worth a given sum doesn't make it so. The real value of any piece of property is only what a ready, willing, and able buyer agrees to pay for it.

So before you plunge headfirst into the world of real estate, make sure you do some serious number crunching. Don't fall into the trap of those who are so eager to buy a piece of property that they fail to examine the true cost of acquiring and holding such an investment. Be sure you carefully weigh every cost associated with buying property, including a host of bank fees, closing costs, transfer taxes, brokerage commissions, and required escrow amounts when you finance your acquisition. If you're trying to purchase rental property, make sure that the rental income to be generated will be adequate to cover the property's mortgage (including principal and interest), taxes, insurance, and operating expenses.

Always Know Your City's Vacancy Rate

By all means factor into your projections realistic setbacks, such as vacancies that affect every building. Only rookie real estate investors assume that their buildings will be occupied 100 percent of the time. Ongoing layoffs across corporate America drive many would-be renters back home with their parents, or into roommate arrangements, both of which boost vacancy rates. Additionally, relatively low interest rates are a factor in higher vacancy rates because low interest rates encourage people to leave the renter's market and opt for homeownership instead. You have to consider how this will affect you in a number of ways. Having fewer renters influences supply and demand. When you're competing with other landlords for a limited pool of tenants, you may be limited in the amount of rent you can charge. So factor this into your profit projections as well.

> **Always factor into your projections potential setbacks**

There's a quick way to gauge whether there's a tenant shortage in your area. Check out the U.S. Census Bureau's Web site (www.census.gov). It contains statistics on vacancy rates for 75 of the largest metropolitan areas in the country. As of this writing, vacancy rates were as low as 3.6 percent in Orange County, CA, and 3.7 percent in Bergen-Passaic, NJ; and as high as 18.5 percent in Atlanta, GA; 18.6 percent in the Raleigh-Durham-Chapel Hill region of North Carolina, and 18.9 percent in Columbus, OH.

How To Start Making Money in Real Estate

If you've ever bought or sold a home, you already know that being in the right location is the number one rule of real estate. We've all heard real estate agents proclaim that "location, location, location" is the most important factor that drives prices. And that's true. But if you're going to purchase property for investment purposes, you'd be wise to also remember this mantra: "diversification, diversification, diversification." Let's say you've assessed all the risks and evaluated the drawbacks, and now you're ready to jump into the world of real estate investing.

Is it good enough to have one piece of property and call it a day? "Many people think owning a duplex somewhere is doing well," says Leo Wells, president of Wells Real Estate Funds in Atlanta. But Wells and other real estate pros say that, to become a successful real estate investor, you must diversify five ways: geographically, by tenant, by tenant industry, by lease term, and by property sector. Don't make the mistake that most real estate novices make when they buy a single piece of property and count on that investment to balance out their portfolios. The idea is to spread out your risk as much as possible, because, "No matter how smart you are, you won't be able to predict which areas will remain strong 10 years from now," said Wells, whose company manages $7 billion in real estate assets and serves more than 200,000 investors.

Cutting Out Responsibilities with REITs

If you don't want the headache and responsibility of personally managing a real estate investment—that means collecting rents, dealing with leaky faucets, and screening tenants—your best bet is to hire a professional property manager or buy real estate through a real estate investment trust, or REIT. REITs are publicly traded companies that own portfolios of real estate investments, including apartment buildings, shopping malls, hotels, offices, and industrial buildings. As exchange-listed entities, REITs have volatility like other stocks, but they more closely resemble mutual funds than individual companies.

The reason a REIT makes sense for most real estate investors is the same reason a mutual fund does: you probably don't want to manage individual properties any more than you want to spend your days and nights looking after the 100 or so individual companies in your mutual fund. Most REIT income is derived from rents, and REITs are required to distribute at least 90 percent of their earnings to their shareholders every year. Wells's company is one such REIT. It builds and manages suburban buildings that will be occupied by Fortune 500 companies that agree to 10-year leases. Investors essentially act as the bank, putting up the money for construction. Wells pays the investors a 7 to 8 percent annual dividend, and the investors own the building. When the building is sold, investors also get any capital appreciation. The company's typical investment size is in the $10 million to $20 million range, but an individual in the Wells Funds can invest as little as $1,000 to $2,000.

Investing in Real Estate Operating Companies

An alternative to investing in REITs is to invest in a real estate operating company. These function essentially in the same business as REITs: building, developing, managing, or leasing properties. But real estate operating companies are generally C corporations or other corporate entities that don't get the special tax status afforded REITs. As a result, real estate operating companies don't have to pay out their cash flow to shareholders in the form of dividends as REITs are required to do by law. For investors in today's market, the trick is finding those solid, top-performing REITs and real estate operating companies. That's where stellar fund managers come in.

Morningstar, a mutual fund information service, can give you performance rankings of the best funds over multiple periods, such as 1-year, 5-year or 10-year returns. Michael Winer, the portfolio manager of the Third Avenue Real Estate Value Fund, which invests in real estate operating companies, once told me that: "Our whole investment philosophy can be summed up in two words: safe and cheap." By safe, he meant that his firm invested only in companies with solid management teams, great track records, and businesses with financial statements that they could understand. The companies also had to have very strong balance sheets, to be able to weather eventual economic downturns. You'd be wise to emulate that strategy, considering Winer's fund, which launched in September 1998, has been red-hot since its inception, ranking among Morningstar's top performers in its category.

Since real estate is a very capital-intensive business, real estate operating companies can retain cash flow and reinvest it back in the business by, say, developing existing properties or making new acquisitions. "I believe this is a distinct advantage of real estate operating companies over REITs," Winer noted, adding that, in order for a REIT to grow, it often has to sell new shares. Most individual investors probably can't go wrong by owning a bit of both. Stick with real estate operating companies to find great real estate values, and purchase REITs for the dividends they'll put in your pocket.

Investing in Housing Tax Credits

Another little-known method for making money in real estate—without becoming a landlord—is to purchase housing tax credits, which can reduce your taxes every year for the following decade.

Although investors have rushed to the real estate arena in recent years, owing in part to a lackluster stock market, relatively few individual investors know about opportunities that exist in the $4 billion housing tax credit industry.

Investing in tax credits is a real estate play that can slash your tax bill, diversify your portfolio, and give you a fairly predictable rate of return for your money. When you invest in housing tax credits, you also fulfill a socially desirable goal: helping to increase the nation's badly needed supply of quality, affordable housing. The lack of adequate housing in America (demand outstrips supply by three to one) has long had an impact on low-income citizens. But recent U.S. census data indicate the severe housing shortage is also beginning to ensnare the middle class. The federal government says there is an unmet demand for nearly 5 million units of clean, affordable housing. So if you're a socially conscious investor, you'll be pleased to know that you can help alleviate an enormous social problem by investing in housing tax credits—and fatten your bank account in the process.

HOW TAX CREDITS WORK

Congress created the Low Income Housing Tax Credit program two decades ago as part of the Tax Reform Act of 1986. The act gave states the power to issue tax credits for the acquisition, rehabilitation, or new construction of rental housing for lower-income residents. These credits became permanent with the passage of the Omnibus Budget Reconciliation Act of 1993. Each state currently receives a tax credit allocation of $1.75 per resident, or a minimum of $42 million for small states such as Rhode Island or Delaware. State housing finance agencies, or other designated state offices, award the tax credits to real estate developers who must submit market studies and competitive proposals for projects aimed at building affordable housing.

These developers, in turn, sell the tax credits to private investors via syndicators. A tax credit syndication firm does due diligence on real estate projects, offers advisory and asset management services, and puts together the limited partnerships through which individuals and corporations invest in community housing.

LOOK FOR A PROVEN TRACK RECORD AND REPUTATION

If you're buying housing tax credits, make sure you check out the track record and reputation of the syndicator, because this firm is pivotal to the success of the deal. According to industry sources, some of the leading national syndicators are: Boston Capital Corp., Columbia Housing Partners of Portland, OR, and Simpson Housing Solutions LLC of Long Beach, CA. Two well-known nonprofit tax syndicators are Enterprise Social Investment Corporation and National Equity Fund. The money raised by the syndication becomes equity in the residential real estate project, lowering borrowing costs and subsidizing tenant rents. These apartment complexes must rent at least 40 percent of their units to tenants whose incomes are 60 percent or less than the median for their region. Also, these housing developments must maintain their low-income rental status for 15 years.

ADVANTAGES FOR INVESTORS

As an investor in housing tax credits, you get a dollar-for-dollar reduction in your tax liability for 10 years. A tax credit is far more valuable than a tax deduction, which only cuts your taxable income. For instance, a $10,000 deduction for a taxpayer in the 35 percent tax bracket will result in a tax savings of $3,500. By contrast, investing in a $10,000 tax credit will put $10,000 back in your wallet—by reducing your taxes by $1,000 a year for a decade. This tax break is one of the few remaining ways in which individuals can shelter taxes. Currently, institutional investors dominate the housing tax credit market. More than 90 percent of all tax credits are now bought by corporate investors, including DaimlerChrysler, Fannie Mae, Freddie Mac, and nearly every major bank. Why would corporations want tax credits? These tax credits aid corporate investors in several ways. They help a company's balance sheet. Additionally, banks can use tax credits to meet their requirements under the Community Reinvestment Act.

Businesses also benefit by improving the neighborhoods in which they operate. Moreover, housing tax credits generate paper or passive losses from depreciation of the underlying buildings.

Companies don't have any limitations on their abilities to use tax credits and passive losses. But for individuals, "The law says you can't reduce your taxes on the last $25,000 of your income," says Boston Capital Securities Inc. president Richard DeAgazio. The tax due on $25,000 for someone in the 28 percent tax bracket is $7,000. "In order to realize that $7,000 tax reduction, you'd make a $70,000 tax credit investment," DeAgazio explains. Also, individuals can use only passive losses to offset passive income—something most individuals generally don't have. Passive income is income generated by activities or businesses in which you don't materially participate, such as rental real estate.

A final benefit to investing in housing tax credits is that limited partnership investors get the profits, if any, that are derived from the sale of the apartment homes—but only after the 15-year compliance period.

DISADVANTAGES TO HOUSING TAX CREDITS

There are several drawbacks to tax credit investing that you should carefully consider. First, you won't typically get the full credit in the first or second year of your investment since there is usually a phase-in period for building low-income housing. The 10-year clock starts ticking once the property is placed in service. Some extra paperwork at tax time can also be a hassle. That isn't a problem, though, if you stick with some of the biggest syndicators because they typically fill out the K-1 form and other tax forms required by the IRS. Boston Capital, for example, does more than 2,000 tax returns each year, including K-1 forms, according to DeAgazio. Illiquidity is another negative factor because there is a very limited secondary market for these partnerships.

You should also pay attention to the front-end fees associated with these projects. The offering costs on a limited-partnership syndication can range from 15 to 28 percent of the money raised, including selling commissions of about 6 to 8 percent to brokers, marketing fees in the 1.5 to 5 percent range, and a host of legal and organizational expenses. But the biggest risk is that the property "falls out of compliance" which makes your tax credits subject to recapture. Examples of noncompliance would be if the property manager rented units to the wrong tenants, charged more rent than legally permissible, or failed to meet mortgage obligations and went into foreclosure.

Noncompliance "is awful because the IRS makes you give back those credits, and you have to go back and refile, pay extra taxes, penalties, and interest," says Duncan Meaney, president of Social Equity Group, a Berkeley, CA, registered investment adviser specializing in socially responsible investing. Fortunately, experts say that noncompliance is infinitesimally small. And even when it does occur, developers get a "cure period" to fix any problems. Still, it is a good idea to know who is managing the property on a day-to-day basis and who is responsible for correcting any mistakes.

As an investor, you want to be certain that the housing complex has been carefully underwritten to make sure that the debt service can be paid. If you follow these tips, you'll be handsomely rewarded with your tax credit investment. While it takes time to get the full payoff, buying housing tax credits comes about as close to getting a guaranteed return as you can get in a real estate investment.

Big Returns with Tax Lien Certificates

If you think housing tax credits are obscure, then you might know even less about the arcane world of property tax lien certificates, an area in which the profits are guaranteed regardless of economic conditions, rising or falling property values, interest rates, or other factors that usually affect real estate profits.

In a nutshell, here's how investing in tax lien certificates works: When a homeowner fails to pay some or all of his or her property taxes, by law, the county must place a lien on the property for the amount that is in default. County governments, like all municipalities, need tax money to finance everything from road repairs to construction of schools and hospitals. In order to avoid having big debts or constantly running a deficit to make up for tax revenue shortfalls, counties offer tax liens for sale to the public, usually through an auction. Should you buy one of these liens, what you're really doing is paying the county the delinquent taxes that are due. Now the property owner owes you the tax money—along with interest on the back taxes. In the vast majority of cases, the property owner comes up with the money and pays his or her obligation. As an investor, you get your money back plus interest that ranges from 8 to 50 percent, depending on the state in which the tax delinquency occurred. If for some reason, the homeowners can't pay or refuse to do so, the property is yours. Since tax liens returns are guaranteed by the government, this is a savvy way to lock in guaranteed real estate profits. And if you really hit the jackpot, you may acquire a piece of property for just the cost of taxes owed on it. Not a bad deal.

How To Profit from Real Estate Foreclosures

Let's turn our discussion away from indirect forms of owning property to a more hands-on approach to investing in real estate. I know that many of you are interested in buying property at bargain-basement prices, especially if you can find such property in the foreclosure market. So let me touch upon this subject, offering you some general advice about how you can profit from real estate foreclosures. Start by thinking about where you want to hunt down foreclosed properties. In general, there are three foreclosure markets:

1. **PROPERTIES IN THE PREFORECLOSURE PHASE:** This happens after the lender files a notice of default. As an investor, you can buy directly from the homeowner at this time.

2. **PROPERTIES UP FOR GRABS AT PUBLIC AUCTION OR SHERIFF/ TRUSTEE SALES:** You can also buy here, usually at the county courthouse.

3. **PROPERTIES IN THE POSTFORECLOSURE PHASE:** If no one bids on a property, the bank takes it back into its inventory. Such property is is commonly known as real estate owned (REO)property. With properties like these, you'll find that bankers are willing to negotiate price, financing, and closing costs.

WHERE TO FIND FORECLOSED PROPERTIES

After you settle on a target location, you should be aware that there are many sources you can utilize to find specific foreclosure deals. Real estate agents are close to the ground, so to speak, and thus are frequently among the first to know about who in the neighborhood lost a job, who died, or who might be going through a divorce—all common reasons for a house to fall into foreclosure. Besides real estate professionals, a host of government and related agencies offer foreclosure properties.

These entities include the Department of Housing and Urban Development (HUD), the Department of Veterans Affairs (VA), the Internal Revenue Service, Federal National Mortgage Association (Fannie Mae), and county tax offices. HUD (www.hud.gov) takes title to between 60,000 and 70,000 homes each year, and HUD homes can sell for anywhere from 10 to 60 percent below market value. True bar-

gains are harder to find these days though, but you can probably find the cheapest-priced buildings among HUD's listing of "uninsured homes." This classification basically means that a home needs so many repairs that it's not eligible for Federal Housing Administration (FHA) financing. So, unless you're ultra handy or have great relationships with reliable contractors who can renovate such a property, think twice before you go after one of these "bargains."

For HUD homes, the FHA doesn't provide any financing; you pay cash or get a mortgage to get the deal done. Fannie Mae, however, does offer financing for many properties. It doesn't loan you money directly. However, Fannie Mae invests in the mortgages that lenders make, providing a constant supply of mortgage dollars to the public. Fannie Mae is publicly traded on the New York Stock Exchange and operates pursuant to a federal charter. This agency originates 25 percent of all home loans in the United States. Its properties are marketed through local brokers, or sometimes directly. For more information visit Fannie Mae's Web site at www.fanniemae.com.

IRS homes that have been foreclosed are sold in "as is" condition. Inspections before the sale are allowed, giving you a chance to get a thorough look at any property you might want to acquire. All IRS properties have a six-month right of redemption. To check out IRS foreclosures, go online to www.treas.gov, and then follow the links to seized property auctions and real estate. The final four sources where you can obtain foreclosure listings are banks with REO departments; services that sell foreclosure listings for a fee (many of these are online); local newspaper ads announcing foreclosure sales; and ads you place directly soliciting sellers facing foreclosure.

EVALUATING FORECLOSURE PROPERTIES

When you evaluate any potential deals, stick to buildings that are structurally sound; avoid those with major structural or environmental problems such as severe foundation settling or extensive roof damage. Also avoid buildings in need of extensive lead paint, asbestos or radon abatement, or any properties where there's been heavy chemical contamination of soil or a contaminated drinking-water supply. Curing these defects usually represents far more trouble than they're worth. In any foreclosure opportunity, make sure you get a good deal going in. In other words, seek out properties that are already priced 20 percent or more below market value. That way you don't have to bank on price appreciation to make the deal financially sound. Do your homework and know the laws governing foreclosures in your state.

With many mortgages, the borrower has a "right of redemption," This means that the homeowner has a certain amount of time to bring the loan current and avoid losing the property through foreclosure. The right of redemption after the sale of property at auction could be as short as one month or as long as one year, as is the case in Alabama and Kansas, respectively. In some states, like New Mexico, the mandatory redemption period precedes the sale, mitigating the risk that the homeowner will come in after a sheriff's sale and reclaim the home.

Which Is Best: Residential or Commercial Real Estate?

If you decide to venture into direct forms of property ownership, in the foreclosure arena or just in the traditional open market, some of you may be wondering where the best returns from real estate are to be reaped: in the residential or commercial market. The truth is that nobody knows how well—or how poorly—real estate will fare in any given year. And if someone claims he or she does, beware. But a study by Lend Lease, an Atlanta real estate management and advisory firm, showed that, historically, real estate has experienced far fewer years of negative returns than stocks and bonds.

Since 1934, returns for real estate have been negative 5 percent of the time, versus about 25 percent of the time for stocks and bonds, according to Lend Lease, which operates in more than 40 countries and has $12 billion in assets under management. The fact that real estate fared well most years was little solace to those hurt by the real estate market downturn in the early 1990s. At that time, the residential and commercial real estate markets both suffered as homeowners were forced to sell middle-class and high-end residences at substantial losses and as changing tax laws wiped out many benefits for real estate investors.

These days, there are still fears about a possible real estate "bubble" as well as worries about the impact of a recession on the real estate market. Despite all these concerns, real estate remains a very viable investment and a very strong leg of the U.S. economy. Additionally, relatively lower interest rates have made it easier than ever to obtain financing, if needed, to buy real property. While rates on 30-year fixed-rate mortgages for principal residences are currently around 7 percent, investor loans are usually about a point higher. The reason banks charge higher rates for these loans is that investment properties typically have more delinquencies and problems than do loans for primary residences. Even though there's lots of money to be lent for real estate, don't just jump at every deal that comes your way. Focus exclusively on those deals that make economic sense. Some experts recommend retail strip centers and shopping malls for individuals seeking diversification. Since these properties have many tenants, investing in a strip mall is akin to the concept of buying into a mutual fund.

Whether you focus on commercial or residential property, just realize that any buildings you buy will sink or swim based on the mix of tenants who occupy the property. In the end, the better your tenants are at paying on time, the stronger your cash flow will be and the fewer problems you will experience. So make sure you rent only to strong, creditworthy tenants—whether you're dabbling in residential or commercial properties.

Commercial real estate loans are for the purchase, new construction, or refinancing of commercial or industrial investment property. Some banks also consider any loan made for investment purposes to fall under the heading of "commercial"—even if it's a residential building you're purchasing. With commercial loans, you can usually get financing for up to 75 percent of the property's value, and the terms last for up to 25 years. As with residential mortgages, commercial real estate loans can have fixed or adjustable interest rates. If you are in the market for a commercial loan, you'll find that in order to finance an income-producing property, such as a strip mall or apartment building, bankers will want to see that the property has enough cash flow to repay the loan. In addition to examining your finances and creditworthiness, a bank is also likely to want to evaluate the financial integrity of the tenants—particularly if the property is largely or exclusively supported by one tenant, such as a commercial warehouse. In some cases, environmental audits and updated rent rolls may be required. These protect the lender against possible contamination at the site or deadbeat tenants.

VALUE IN LOW-END RESIDENTIAL

Building trends in most metropolitan areas nationwide suggest that redeveloping urban centers is a strategy gaining in popularity. No doubt it's riskier too, because you really have to know the fundamentals of a local neighborhood to say with any degree of certainty whether or not it will "come back" in a year or two. But, while the risks are greater, so are the financial rewards, as I experienced with my land deal in Newark. In recent times, the same has held true in other markets, such as the Pontiac and Detroit areas of Michigan, where investors in the residential market routinely earn double-digit returns on properties in the $250,000 and under range.

Despite the potential gains, some of you may not be inclined to venture into urban areas that may (or may not) be on the verge of a turnaround. If that describes you, another strategy might be to buy on the fringes of an area where development is heavy.

Let's say you know of a district where real estate pros are buying property left and right or rehabbing every other building on the block. Well, your strategy would be to buy commercial property two or three blocks away from the center of activity. This way you benefit from the economic development taking place. After all, when construction is heightened in a region, there's a ripple effect that permeates throughout the larger neighborhood. And this boom in activity spells opportunity for smart investors.

When you buy on the fringes, chances are you'll acquire real estate that's less expensive than where the action is "hot." That's a definite plus. One drawback, though, is that you have to realize that while the highly developed areas might grow, at say, 10 or 20 percent a year, your investment in a "fringe" property will probably not keep pace with the same level of growth. Nevertheless, it will still grow. Last, if you're going to focus on buy and hold properties—those you'll keep for appreciation over the long run—make sure you have an adequate cash cushion. Remember that all tenants won't pay on time, that you'll incur ordinary costs in the course of holding and running these buildings, and that unexpected expenses will pop up as well.

A Home of Your Own

We've talked a lot about real estate investments that are not your primary residence. Now I think it's time to offer some guidance to those of you who are simply trying to buy your own home—perhaps a first house. Fortunately, you can build wealth this way too. And while it can be a hardship to come up with the necessary down payment to buy a home, getting your own piece of the American dream doesn't have to be out of your reach. In decades past, a would-be home buyer who wanted to purchase a home had to fork over 20 percent of the value of that property. That large chunk of money represented a huge obstacle to homeownership, especially since the down payment didn't include all the closing costs you pay—points, appraisal costs, lawyers fees, and so on—when buying real estate. Thankfully, it's easier nowadays than ever to go from renter to homeowner without having to come up with a 20 percent down payment.

With the help of a few agencies, including the Federal Housing Administration, you can buy a home for 5 percent, or even as little as 3 percent, down. In some cases no money down deals are available in which you receive 100 percent financing. The FHA doesn't lend you money. But it does guarantee your mortgage. When you get an FHA-backed mortgage, the FHA promises your lender—doesn't matter if it's a bank, savings and loan, credit union, or another institution—that if you default on the loan for any reason, the FHA will step in, pay off the mortgage, and take over the house.

Qualifying for an FHA-insured loan is fairly straightforward. You must have satisfactory credit. You must be able to pay your closing costs, roughly 3 percent of the cost of the house, excluding points. You must show the FHA that you have steady income and will be able to make your payments. The house must be up to code and "suitably located as to site and neighborhood." Besides the low down payment, one major plus to FHA-backed loans is that they're often offered at lower interest rates than conventional, or nongovernmental, mortgages.

But getting an FHA-backed loan has some drawbacks, too. One of the disadvantages of an FHA-insured mortgage is that you must obtain mortgage insurance, and it's not cheap. Currently, the insurance costs 2.25 percent of the amount the FHA is guaranteeing. First-time home buyers, however, can get their mortgage insurance premium rate reduced to 1.75 percent if they take a housing counseling class. Even so, the cost of mortgage insurance, payable at settlement, can usually be spread out over your monthly payments. Another downside to getting an FHA-insured mortgage is that there is a limit to the amount the agency will insure. Effective January 1, 2006, the FHA began insuring single-family home mortgages up to $200,160 in standard areas and up to $362,790 in high-cost areas. While that represented a 15 percent increase over the previous year's loan limits, rising property values mean that some buyers who qualify for an FHA-backed loan are nevertheless priced out of the market.

If you are a veteran, you may be able to get an even better deal. The Veterans Administration backs 0 percent down mortgages for qualified applicants. VA-insured loans offer other benefits as well. For example, leniency is extended to VA homeowners experiencing a temporary cash crunch. Despite their appeal, there are negative aspects to VA-guaranteed loans as well. One drawback is that the Veterans Administration won't guarantee adjustable-rate mortgages (ARMS). Additionally, it costs you 2 percent of the mortgage to get a VA-insured loan. A VA home buyer must pay a 1 percent "funding fee" to the government, and another 1 percent "origination fee" to the lender. Even if you're seeking a conventional loan that's not backed by the FHA or VA, you can still get around a high down payment. The mortgage lending business is extremely competitive. Banks, mortgage brokers, and others know that customers shop around. As a result, it's fairly easy to find an institution that will finance your mortgage if you make a 5 or 10 percent down payment. The better your credit rating and the more solid your overall application, the better off you'll be in negotiating with a lender.

Of course, there's no free ride, so be aware that anyone securing a conventional loan and putting down less than 20 percent for a home usually pays what's known as private mortgage insurance (PMI). The cost of PMI, usually 2 to 3 percent of the loan, is tacked onto the cost of your mortgage, and you typically pay this fee monthly. One of the drawbacks to PMI loans is that they sometimes involve tougher lending standards. Your total housing cost—principal, interest, taxes, and insurance—can't exceed 28 percent of your income. By comparison, with FHA loans, your housing costs can represent 35 percent of your income. Also, some PMI lenders require that the down payment funds come exclusively from the home buyer; in other words, none of the money can be a gift from your mother, father, or anyone else.

Clearly, there are many pros and cons to getting a mortgage via the FHA, VA, or PMI lenders. The important point to remember, however, is that through all these institutions you can pay far less than a 20 percent down payment for the home of your dreams. Finally, if you do buy a house and pay less than 20 percent down, remember to have your lender eliminate your mortgage insurance charges once you've built up 20 percent equity in your home. Lenders often overlook this charge on older loans, so you must be vigilant about this and specifically direct them to stop charging you for PMI once you build up 20 percent equity in your home.

Tapping into Your Home Equity

Speaking of tapping your home's equity, many older Americans, however, may be sitting on a ready supply of tax-free money just waiting to be tapped in the form of a reverse mortgage. What's more, the cash you can generate with a reverse mortgage isn't tied to the ups and downs in the financial markets—a big bonus for those squeamish about continued stock market volatility or investors who have seen their dividend income dwindle in recent years. Reverse mortgages are little-understood loans made to individuals at least 62 years old with substantial equity in their homes. These loans differ from conventional mortgages and traditional home equity loans in that instead of your making a regular monthly payment to the bank, the bank pays you a fixed amount of money each month. Actually, reverse mortgage loans can come in the form of a lump-sum payment, monthly installments, a line of credit, or some combination of these.

You can use the money for anything you want—including paying off bills, traveling, or making home repairs and improvements. You retain the title and deed to your property. The loan gets repaid when you die or sell your home. Getting a reverse mortgage isn't dependent upon your credit. Plus, there are no income requirements, and applicants don't have to take any kind of medical exams. The size of the loan and any monthly payment you can get depend on several factors including your life expectancy, current interest rates, the equity you have built up in your home and whether you're in a high-cost, modest or less expensive section of the country.

Elderly homeowners have been known to use reverse mortgages to do everything from fixing up their homes to purchasing supplemental insurance. One bonus to reverse mortgages is that the bank's payments to you are guaranteed for as long as you live in your home. If you should live longer than the bank's actuaries predicted, the lender must still continue making payments to you.

INDUSTRY SEEN MUSHROOMING

A handful of recent events has made reverse mortgages more attractive than ever. As mentioned earlier, the Federal Housing Administration, the biggest sponsor of reverse mortgages and an arm of the U.S. Department of Housing and Urban Development, on January 1, 2006, increased the loan limits for these and other mortgage products. The FHA reverse mortgage is called a home equity conversion mortgage (HECM) and can be obtained through local lenders. The second largest provider of reverse mortgages, the Federal National Mortgage Association, also upped its loan limits effective January 1, 2006. Fannie Mae's new guidelines permit loans as high as $417,000. Fannie Mae's reverse mortgage offering is known as "Home Keeper." The Home Keeper loan is similar to the FHA's HECM product in that both are offered through local lenders.

If you happen to be a homeowner who is particularly house rich, but cash poor, you might turn to financial institutions such as Financial Freedom of Irvine, CA, which offers two so-called jumbo reverse mortgage products, providing loans up to $1 million for upscale borrowers. Company officials say clients who get these jumbo loans sometimes use the reverse mortgage as tax and estate-planning tools. All monies received from reverse mortgages are tax-free since you're really just borrowing against existing equity in your home. Every year, reverse mortgages are growing in popularity. "As baby boomers reach retirement age, these products will become as common as mutual funds," says Peter Bell, president of the nonprofit National Reverse Mortgage Lenders Association in Washington, DC. The trade group's members originate and service more than 90 percent of all reverse mortgages. Those members sign a code of conduct pledging to abide by guidelines that ensure fair, ethical, and respectful practices in offering and making reverse mortgages to seniors.

In addition to larger loan limits, another reason reverse mortgages are expected to gain in popularity is that more states are beginning to permit these products. So far, HECM or Home Keeper loans can be obtained in practically every state in the country. Meanwhile, roughly 180 firms nationally make reverse mortgage loans, according to Bell.

LOANS HAVE CERTAIN DRAWBACKS

Like all financial products, reverse mortgages have their disadvantages. There are three main drawbacks to getting a reverse mortgage. The first is that senior citizens say these loans can be complicated, requiring a lot of paperwork. Adding to the complexity, reputable lenders require that you get counseling before taking out these loans. So you'll need to find two people to help you with the process: a reverse mortgage counselor and a reverse mortgage lender. And, unfortunately, not all mortgage representatives are familiar with the ins and outs of reverse mortgages.

For FHA-backed loans, HUD-approved nonprofit groups provide counseling on reverse mortgages. To find a counselor in your area, contact HUD's Housing Counseling Clearinghouse at (800) 569-4287 or go to www.hud.gov. Fannie Mae also does in-person counseling and provides guidance over the telephone when borrowers are more than 40 miles away from a counseling center. To find a lender, you can go to the Web site for the National Reverse Mortgage Loan Association (www.reversemortgage.org). An additional drawback is that obtaining a reverse mortgage can be relatively expensive—on the order of 4 percent of the loan, including fees and insurance.

Generally, you'll incur the same types of charges that are found when you get a conventional mortgage, including origination, appraisal, and local recording fees. However, past legislation capped the origination fee—that's what the lender earns in the form of points—at $2,000 or 2 percent of the maximum loan amount, whichever is greater. You may also have to pay a 2 percent mortgage insurance premium to HUD if the FHA is offering insurance to back the loan. While all the fees are ultimately paid out of the loan proceeds so that there's no out-of-pocket cash required for the entire transaction, you should still be aware that all the costs involved can add up.

One final negative aspect is that, depending on the size and structure of the reverse mortgage you get, your home may have to be sold upon your death to pay back the bank. This could be an obstacle if you were hoping to leave your residence to your children or other heirs. On the bright side, though, since reverse mortgages are "nonrecourse" loans, nobody will ever pay back more than the value of the home. Also, if your home does rise in value while you have a reverse mortgage, and then you die, the bank will seek to be repaid only for the value of your loan. Any additional funds reaped from the sale will go to your heirs, who effectively benefit from your home's price appreciation.

Your Own Net Worth

Now that you have a host of ideas about how you can leverage real estate to suit your needs, let's look at how real estate may be part of your current net worth. Even if you don't currently own any property, the next exercise is designed to teach you how to calculate your net worth. In its simplest terms, your net worth is defined as everything you own (your assets) minus everything you owe (your liabilities). When you list everything, it can be a real eye-opener. So take a moment and figure out your own net worth, using the following form taken from America Saves (www.americasaves.org). It's one of the best summary statements I've found anywhere and lets you quickly and easily estimate your net worth and get a snapshot of your financial strength.

After you add up all your assets, tally up your debts and subtract them from the total of your assets. Hopefully, it's a positive number. If not, it means you presently have a negative net worth. Should that be the case, you definitely have your work cut out for you. But don't feel for a second that you're destined to be in the red forever. It's not uncommon at all for people to experience big swings in their net worth once they start shoring up their finances. And certainly once you begin making real estate a part of your asset base, you'll be in the black sooner than you know it.

ESTIMATING YOUR CURRENT NET WORTH
Supply the following information in order to estimate your current net worth:

FINANCIAL ASSETS

Bank/Credit Union Checking and/or
Savings Accounts (current balances) $_____

Certificates of Deposits (CDs) and
U.S. Savings Bonds (current balances) $_____

IRAs (current balances/assets) $_____

Stocks/Mutual Funds (current assets) $_____

Retirement Plan—401k, 403b, STRS,
profit-sharing (current assets) $_____

Life Insurance—whole, variable and
universal (current cash value) $_____

NON-FINANCIAL ASSETS

House(s)/Other Real Estate
(current market value) $_____

Car(s)/Truck(s)/Recreation Vehicle (s)
(current value) $_____

Other—boats, motorcycles, furniture,
appliances, collectibles (current value) $_____

DEBTS

*Installment—auto, furniture, appliances
(combined balances owed)* $_____

Credit Cards (combined balances owed) $_____

*First Home Mortgage
(remaining principal owed)* $_____

*Second Mortgage/Home Equity Loan
(amount owed)* $_____

*Loans from Retirement Plan
(combined balances owed)* $_____

Other Debts (combined amounts owed) $_____

SOURCE: America Saves, a nationwide coalition of nonprofit, corporate and government groups.

Is Your Home an Asset?

Some of you may find that your home is your biggest financial asset. And make no mistake, your home is definitely an asset. I know you may have heard others suggest that it isn't, based on the theory that an asset is anything that puts money into your pocket, not takes money out of your pocket, as is the case when you're paying a mortgage on your home. But let me offer three arguments that unequivocally demonstrate how your house is an asset. For starters, unlike a paper asset (such as a stock), you don't have to wait to sell your house in order to reap financial rewards from it. Can you not tap into the equity in your house (without selling) and cash out thousands upon thousands of dollars? This money is yours to use any way you see fit, whether you buy a new car or boat or invest in additional real estate. And what about when you actually do sell your home, if you've been paying down that mortgage (as should be the case) and the market has risen in your area (as hopefully is the case), you should earn a profit from the sale of that home. Those are real dollars; not phantom profits. And finally, I challenge you to walk into any bank in the country and try to get a loan. The bank will check your credit and ask for a list of your financial assets and liabilities.

From Maine to New Mexico and from Seattle to Syracuse, I guarantee you'd be hard-pressed to find a single banker who doesn't count your home—specifically the equity you have in your home—as part of your net worth. So if the banks count your home as an asset, why shouldn't you? In the introduction to this book, I cited a survey which revealed that there are 8.9 million millionaire households in the United States. Well, again, that study referred to wealthy households with $1 million in assets *excluding* their primary residences. When you count principal residences as part of net worth, the number of millionaires in this country is substantially higher. So, no matter what your net worth statement shows as of today, just know that by leveraging the power of property, you're one step closer to joining the millionaire ranks.

5

INCREASE YOUR FORTUNE
WITH PROVEN METHODS,
NOT SHORTCUTS

The managing director of Chartered Financial Analyst Institute, Robert Johnson, will never forget the time he was giving a financial presentation in Louisville, Kentucky, during the height of the Internet investing boom. Johnson was espousing the value of the CFA organization and talking about how to value a company based on traditional investment criteria—such as using discounted cash flows—when a fellow in the audience stood up and said that the CFA program was passé.

According to this gentleman, it was foolish to use old-school methodologies to figure out how much new-age technology companies were worth. "If you use that logic," the man told Johnson, "a lot of these Internet companies wouldn't be worth anything." That's exactly my point, Johnson thought. Ultimately, when the Internet bubble burst and scores of dot-com companies went bust, investors finally realized that too. The tech meltdown that began in early 2000 is a constant reminder to veteran investors like Johnson about why groups such as the CFA Institute—which counts 80,000 financial professionals among its ranks—value proven investment strategies above all else. "Nothing gets in the CFA program until it's tried and true," Johnson says. "When you get right down to it, there may be new products, new funds, and things, but in terms of what ultimately creates value, it's been the same forever." I couldn't agree more because I don't believe in reinventing the wheel— especially when it comes to making money.

I'd much prefer to go with proven methods to fatten my bank account rather than rely on so-called "new" money-making strategies, fads, hunches, or speculative get-rich-quick schemes. So if you're going to invest in the public markets to make money, you can save yourself a lot of cash (and a lot of grief) by investing like the pros do—using the wisdom, strategies, and techniques that have made people wealthy decade after decade after decade. And when I say "pros," I mean various people who have been successful investors. Some are professionals by trade, such as stockbrokers, money managers, or traders. But many pros, by my judgment, are investors like you and me—working people who have their own careers, families, and interests. They don't want to spend their lives sitting in front of a computer screen plotting their next stock pick. Nor do they want to watch the gyrations of the Dow Jones Industrial Average on an hour-by-hour basis. And neither should you. Why should you spend countless amounts of time, effort, research, and money trying to figure out how to beat the market when scores of people before you have already been where you are and have laid a trail of bread crumbs for you to follow to successfully navigate your way along Wall Street? These people have left plenty of clues for us to figure out which pathways lead to riches and which are just dead-end roads.

Millionaire Stock Investors

I'm going to let you in on something that millionaire stock investors like Charles Schwab know. The vast majority of them don't spend a whole lot of time researching complicated companies whose businesses they don't understand. They don't make money by using secret investing strategies to which only the rich are privy. And they certainly don't rely on complex formulas, detailed spreadsheets, and sophisticated algorithms to figure out what to buy or sell. Do you know what they do instead? They master the core principles of investing—the straightforward, irrefutable, can't-go-wrong-with-this kind of advice that has worked for eons. Many of the concepts and strategies that guide their activities are based on plain vanilla investing ideas—nothing fancy. But they certainly do work year in and year out. And they certainly can make you wealthy. Just look at the famous billionaire investor Warren Buffett. He says that one of his investing guidelines is to, "Stay with simple propositions." Therefore, as an investor in stocks or bonds, your best bet is to also stick with basic, tried-and-true wisdom—the kind of knowledge that comes as much from seasoned investors educated in the school of hard knocks as from MBA types trained at the likes of Harvard and Yale. Both groups represent some of the best and the brightest in the financial services world. And it's from their collective wisdom that we can all learn the dos and don'ts of investing. It's not about trying to beat the market. And it's not exclusively about buying low and selling high. Investing should be done with a goal in mind. You invest for a purpose—not to just keep score that you "outperformed" this or that index.

10 Lessons from the Top

In this chapter, I reveal 10 lessons I've been fortunate enough to learn as a result of interviewing some of the top minds on Wall Street— as well as everyday individuals who have proven to be remarkably successful at increasing their fortunes with stocks and bonds. I pass these lessons along to you in the hopes that you will use them in your quest for financial freedom. These 10 lessons will not only help you become a millionaire, but they'll also help you sidestep a number of pitfalls as you journey into the fascinating, sometimes wacky, world of Wall Street. After I tell you these lessons and explain how you can use them to build long-lasting wealth, I'll also give you my unique perspective on what it takes to achieve investing success no matter how much experience, money, or financial knowledge you may have.

Lesson 1: Long-Term Investing Trumps Speculating, Market Timing, and Short-Term Trading

Why is it that so many investors jump from one stock to the next without regard for the negative ramifications of buying and selling investments too quickly? Trading too often causes a number of problems. It generates high commissions; which makes brokers richer but takes unnecessary money out of your pocket. When you sell investments held for less than a year, you have to pay higher short-term capital gains taxes, which are imposed at ordinary income tax rates as high as 35 percent. By contrast, holding stock for longer than a year gets you long-term capital gains treatment, which means most investors pay taxes of just 15 percent.

Trading too frequently also causes your investments to underperform over time. Despite all these drawbacks, countless investors persist in trying to time the market, jumping in and out of the market as if investing were akin to watching a spate of TV shows on a Saturday night. Don't like what you see? Then just hit the button and quickly move on to the next program. Such rapid-fire change may give you entertainment satisfaction, but it can be disastrous for your investing portfolio. Much of this frenzied trading activity has been driven by the emergence of online trading and the ease of accessing stock information over the Internet.

Trading too frequently causes your investments to underperform over time.

You remember the explosion of day-trading in the late 1990s, right? Well, most of that crowd soon discovered what folks like Buffett know: that long-term investing ultimately carries the day. That's why Buffett is famous for saying that the best time to sell a stock is *never*. That philosophy typifies his ultrastrong adherence to a buy-and-hold investing strategy. Since I'm assuming you're not quite as independently wealthy as Warren Buffett—who can surely afford to live off the interest alone on his investments—I dare say there will come a time when you'll need to sell some of your shares. Nevertheless, don't take part in the speculative type of trading that is evidenced by investors these days who hold stocks for a remarkably short period of time, despite conventional wisdom that long-term investing produces superior investment returns.

INVESTORS SELL STOCKS FASTER THAN EVER

According to research from Bain & Co., back in 1960, the average holding period for a stock listed on the New York Stock Exchange (NYSE) was 8.3 years. In 1970, investors held Big Board stocks for an average of 5.3 years. By 1980, the typical holding period had dropped to 2.8 years. It fell further to an average of 2.2 years in 1990, and 1.3 years in 2000. Can you guess how long investors these days hang on to shares traded on the NYSE? Just 11 months. That's right, less than one year! As you can see, over time, investors have gotten trigger happy—largely to their own detriment. If you look at the historical returns for stocks, you'll find that for every 10-year period since the 1920s, equities have posted returns averaging 10 percent. These are very respectable returns. But they've only been possible because, even when there have been market downturns, the market has been able to come back and correct itself over time.

Those soft spots in the stock market, therefore, get eroded by the strong bull runs that occur. The problem is that no one can predict exactly when a nice run-up will happen. So instead of hopping in and out of stocks and trying to figure out if there's a market bottom or if the market has peaked, it's far better to stay steadily invested. There's a saying that, "Successful investing is about time invested in the market, and not timing the market." Again, the research bears this out. A study by Ibbotson Associates looked at investment returns for the S&P 500 index for the 10-year period from 1980 through 1989. Ibbotson found that if you stayed invested in the S&P 500 for each one of the 2,528 trading days during that decade, you would have earned 17.5 percent average annual returns. However, if you jumped out of the market on just 10 of the best trading dates of that decade, your average annual return would have fallen to 12.6 percent. Even worse, if you missed the 40 best days of the market during that 10-year span, your return would've amounted to just 3.9 percent. Clearly, this shows the financial damage that can be done by short-term trading or trying to time the market.

Lesson 2: Index Funds Generally Outpace Actively Managed Funds

If you participate in your 401(k) plan at work, or an equivalent retirement savings vehicle, you already know a bit about mutual funds. These are baskets of securities that offer professional money management, diversification, and generally a low-cost way to invest in the stock and bond markets. By purchasing mutual funds, you get a variety of investments that would've been much more costly to acquire individually. Index funds are typically the least expensive of all funds when it comes to fees, since no active management is required. Index funds are passive investments in the sense that when a fund company has an index fund it simply automatically buys the stocks that comprise a certain index, such as the NASDAQ 100. This way, no professional money manager has to do a whole lot of research, analysis, travel, or meeting with corporate management to figure out which companies are great prospects (and therefore "buys") and which ones are dogs (and therefore "sells"). These passively run index funds beat actively managed funds 80 percent of the time, statistics show. So if dedicated money-management professionals, who get paid to live, breathe, eat, and sleep the stock market, still can't outperform the indexes eight out ten times, is it reasonable to expect that you and I will? I don't think so. And it's not any reflection on your intelligence or abilities.

CAN ANYONE CONSISTENTLY BEAT THE ODDS?

It mostly boils down to a numbers game and some fundamentals about how the market works. The simple truth is that actively managed funds have higher marketing costs and fees, along with larger concentrations in certain stocks or industries because the fund manager is paid to pick those stocks he or she thinks will outperform the broader market. When a fund manager bets incorrectly on one of those favored stocks or industries, the actively managed fund's performance suffers. By contrast, with an index fund, you're taking the human element of a fund manager who is making subjective judgments out of the equation, and you're buying equal amounts of all the stocks that represent a given index. In the end, statistics show that these index funds outperform actively managed funds by an average of two percentage points annually. That's a big difference—especially over long periods of time.

Statistics show that index funds outperform actively managed funds by an average of two percentage points annually.

For instance, $10,000 invested in an index fund that earns 10 percent a year over the course of 50 years will result in a gigantic portfolio that hits $1,170,000 in size at the end of those five decades. But if you were in an actively managed fund that returned just 8 percent annually, your $10,000 investment would compound to just $470,000 over 50 years. That's a full $700,000 less because of the 2 percent difference in long-term returns. The bottom line: more often than not, you earn far more with index funds than with actively managed funds. Some of you may be asking: why buy funds at all? Isn't the real action in buying individual stocks? Well, yes and no. If you're talking about pizzazz and excitement, the action may very well be with certain stocks—when you can find them. Every one of us can point to companies that have seen spectacular run-ups in their share price; some big-name stocks have seen triple-digit annual returns. And that makes many investors want to try their hands at individual stock-picking. But doing so is typically a money-losing proposition for most individuals, experts warn.

> Stick to those index funds that spread out your risk and offer the prospect for better long-term returns.

STOP LOOKING FOR THE NEXT MICROSOFT OR GOOGLE

"I tend to believe that most people should stay away from individual stocks unless they're really familiar with the company or the people running the company," says Greg Sullivan, managing director at Harris Bank. "Everyone is looking for that next Microsoft, Cisco, or Google. But they don't realize how many of these companies don't pan out." Indeed, because there is a universe of well over 5,000 publicly traded stocks, why should you rack your brains trying to pick the one or two—or even five, seven or twelve—stocks that could be winners? Stick to those index funds that spread out your risk and offer the prospect for better long-term returns. "Even managed funds are fun and exciting on a year by year basis because they sometimes do very well," says Sullivan. "But with index funds, you'll generally have higher returns in the long run, less stress, and fewer taxes to worry about. There's also less oversight that's necessary, so I recommend index funds for most people if they don't have professional management to work with them."

Lesson 3: No-Load Investments Are Preferable to Funds with Loads

With no-load funds you don't pay any sales charge or commission to buy or sell shares in a mutual fund. (A "load" is a sales charge or commission.) By comparison, you do pay commissions when you invest in funds with sales loads. There are many different types of loads, and you need to be aware of them all. You can tell what kind of commission you'll be charged by the type of shares you purchase in a mutual fund. Class A shares indicate front-end-loaded mutual funds, or ones for which you pay an up-front fee that's deducted from your investment. So if you invest $1,000 in a mutual fund with a 3 percent sales load, this means that $30 of your money is taken out to pay a commission, and just $970 is actually being invested. Class B shares are those with so-called "back-end" loads, meaning you pay no up-front fee, but you do pay a "redemption fee" if you sell before a set time, usually six years. Most B shares convert to A shares after six to ten years. Class C shares are known as "level-load" funds. These don't charge a front- or back-end sales charge. Instead, you pay a higher annual fee.

> **It generally pays to stick to no-load funds because the commissions associated with load funds will turn into a drag on performance over time.**

When you buy a fund with a sales load—no matter whether you purchase Class A, B, or C shares—that sales charge or commission comes on top of another set of fees that all mutual fund shareholders pay. That's because sales charges and commissions are not included in what's called a fund's "expense ratio." A fund's annual expense ratio is the total percentage of the fund's assets used for administrative, advertising, marketing, and other operating expenses. So a fund with an annual expense ratio of 1 percent spends 1 percent of its assets to cover operating expenditures. And that expense ratio excludes sales costs and brokerage commissions.

The commissions on mutual funds with sales loads range from about 1 to 6 percent.

Given a choice between two funds, if all other things are equal—in terms of their performance, holdings, investment style, and objective—it generally pays to stick to no-load funds because the commissions associated with load funds will turn into a drag on performance over time. Despite this fact, a surprising number of investors go for funds with sales charges. Only 13 percent of all new mutual fund sales are made directly between an investor and a fund (mainly no-load funds), down from 23 percent in 1990, according to the Investment Company Institute, a trade group for the mutual fund industry. Collectively, this means that investors are giving up a lot of money in fees unnecessarily. For instance, assume that you and a friend each invested $10,000 in a mutual fund that earns 10 percent for the next 10 years. By the end of that time, you have $23,457, but your friend only has $22,284. What accounts for that $1,173 difference? Your friend bought a front-loaded mutual fund and paid a 5 percent sales charge. So while she made a $10,000 investment, $500 of that went toward an up-front commission, cutting her true initial investment to $9,500. She not only started $500 behind you, she also lost out on earning the compounded interest on that $500.

Lesson 4: Diversification Is Always Better Than Putting All Your Eggs in One Basket

If there's one principle of investing that will serve you well time and time again, it's that you should always—repeat *always*—seek to have a diversified pot of investments. Unfortunately, far too many people fail to heed this conventional wisdom even though it's worked forever for large and small investors alike. Contrary to popular opinion, being diversified isn't solely about buying mutual funds. While it's correct that the average investor will get far better diversification with mutual funds than with individual stocks— after all the typical equity mutual fund holds nearly 200 stocks—it's also true that you can really go awry in your investing strategy if you

> **Always, always, always have diversified investments.**

don't know how to go about achieving proper diversification. Millionaire investors diversify across a number of areas—and so should you.

GETTING YOUR PORTFOLIO PROPERLY DIVERSIFIED

Start by investing across asset class. This means that you won't just invest in stocks, but also in bonds or fixed-income securities, as well as in real estate or other areas that might be appropriate for your individual needs. For some investors, holding a portion of their assets in cash also constitutes proper diversification. But you can't be well diversified if your money is 100 percent in stocks. That's foolish because it really suggests that you're chasing returns—or being greedy in your quest to get returns far above market averages. After you diversify across asset class, make sure you have investments in various market capitalization (cap) ranges.

A stock's market cap is calculated by multiplying the number of shares a company has outstanding by its stock price. So if a publicly traded company you're considering investing in has 50 million shares issued, and the company's shares are selling for $15 apiece, then that firm has a market cap of $750 million. While $750 million might sound like a big number, believe it or not, that's considered a small-cap company. You can ask 10 different people about what constitutes a small-cap, mid-cap or large-cap stock based on size, and you'll probably get 10 different answers. Nevertheless, many experts say that small-cap stocks range anywhere from $300 million to about $1 billion in size; any smaller than that, and you're talking about penny stocks, which are far less liquid and typically have few if any analysts covering them. For mid-cap stocks, the accepted wisdom is that these companies vary in size from roughly $1.5 billion to $8.5 billion. Large-cap stocks are said to be those in excess of $9 billion dollars.

Obviously, there is some overlap, but this is the consensus in terms of how these companies are classified by size. In theory, at least, small-cap stocks offer the most oppor-

Invest in a wide array of sectors—anything from clothing retailers, automotive companies, or other consumer products businesses to leisure and entertainment stocks.

tunity for growth potential. And they often do, in fact, far outpace the annual performance rate of their mid-cap and large-cap brethren. But again, to be properly diversified, you need a bit of each, because you can't always determine which sector will be in favor. In other words, when small-cap stocks are out of favor, large-cap issues may be in vogue and vice versa.

INVESTING ACROSS MULTIPLE INDUSTRIES

Once you diversify across asset class and market cap range, you should think about the myriad industries or sectors you want to hold in your investment portfolio. For example, just because you work in the health-care industry, that doesn't mean that all your investments should be in health-care-related companies. Ditto for banking, insurance, telecommunications, or any other industry you can think of. The idea is to have a wide array of sectors in which you invest—anything from clothing retailers, automotive companies or other consumer products businesses to leisure and entertainment stocks that are found in the hospitality and travel industries.

Who knew that Hurricanes Katrina and Rita would have such a devastating impact on tourism in the South in 2005, 2006 and beyond? The same is true for the September 11 attacks back in 2001, which had a severely negative impact on the airline industry. So to protect yourself from unexpected events and even just normal market downturns, make sure you spread your investments across multiple industries. By the same token, you should invest in multiple companies. Don't tie up all your money in one stock—especially if that stock is the very company you work for. One might think that investors would have learned this lesson after spectacular corporate failures such as Enron, where employees lost everything, particu-

Don't tie up all your money into one stock—diversify!

larly those who had all their retirement monies tied up in Enron stock. But the undesirability of being so heavily invested in company stock is clearly a lesson that has not taken hold for scores of investors.

THE RISKS OF HOLDING TOO MUCH COMPANY STOCK

According to a study by the nonpartisan Employee Benefit Research Institute in Washington, DC, a large percentage of people have 25 percent or more of their 401(k) assets invested in their company's stock. The problem of overinvesting in company stock has gotten so bad that the National Association of Securities Dealers issued an alert to investors warning them about the dangers of this practice. "For some people, a 401(k) plan is their only form of retirement savings," said John Gannon, NASD vice president for investor education. "And they shouldn't gamble their financial security in retirement on the success of just one stock." So forget what you've heard about the Microsoft millionaires or, more lately, the employees of Google who've become millionaires (at least on paper) by holding company stock. It's far too risky a strategy. If your employer's business folds or goes through a serious financial crisis, not only will your job be at risk, but so will your retirement monies. If you want to lessen the risk that your investments will suffer because of poor diversification, strive to invest in both value and growth funds. Value funds or value stocks are those that you try to buy on the cheap.

Warren Buffett is a consummate value investor, purchasing a stock when he believes it's been beaten down, in terms of price, but when the company is nonetheless strong and viable. Growth investors seek double-digit returns from companies they believe have above-average market prospects. Over the years, there's been a constant battle between the performance of value and growth stocks. When one does well, the other tends to do poorly, or at least so-so. Therefore, it pays to have both growth and value funds in your portfolio, and not be wedded exclusively to either style of investing.

To be properly diversified, you also need to expand your investment holdings across geographic boundaries. Far too many U.S. investors buy only domestic securities. That's a big mistake. You can often get better returns, and enhance the diversification in your portfolio, by going beyond North American borders. After you do some homework, consider investing internationally—in developed markets such as Germany or the United Kingdom, along with emerging markets like Thailand or South Africa.

Ultimately, if your investment portfolio contains a nice mix across asset classes; if you've interspersed your investments with small-, mid-, and large-cap stocks; if you've bought a range of stock of different companies in different sectors; if you've purchased both value- and growth-oriented funds; and if you've branched out geographically as well, then—and only then—can you say that you're practicing the tried and true wisdom of having a diversified investment strategy.

Lesson 5: Asset Allocation Is the Primary Factor in Portfolio Performance

Studies show that 90 percent of portfolio performance is determined by asset allocation—or how you divide up your investments. This means that you should be less worried about specific products and more concerned with making sure you've got the right mix of stocks, bonds, cash, and other investments. Too often though, people worry about finding the right individual stocks or bonds to buy. This is a dangerous proposition because individual stocks can experience tremendous bouts of volatility in relatively short periods of time— making it very tough to say which ones will be long-term winners and which will be losers.

GOOGLE'S ROLLER-COASTER RIDE

Google went public on August 19, 2004, at $85 a share. Google quickly became enormously popular on Main Street and Wall Street alike. In fact, the word "Google" has become a verb for those who use the company's search engine to access information on the Internet. Wall Street has fallen in love with Google, as evidenced by the preponderance of analysts who are bullish on the stock and urge investors to buy shares of Google. As a result, Google's shares skyrocketed to an all-time closing high of $471.63 on January 11, 2006. However, by January 20, 2006, Google shares suffered their worst-ever point decline, falling by 8.5 percent in a single day to $399.46. That means that in a span of just eight trading days, Google's shares lost 15 percent of their value.

What caused Google to experience that huge one-day point drop? The company did not disclose any "bad" news. It did not miss earnings expectations. It didn't suffer a drop in advertising revenues. There were no management problems. Instead, Google was a victim of a lot of outside market forces. For starters, one of its competitors released negative news. Yahoo!, the largest Internet media company, stunned investors by posting lower-than-expected earnings results. Additionally, the U.S. Justice Department had issued a subpoena (which Google was resisting) asking Google to turn over search records for a federal case involving antipornography law. And, finally, a brokerage firm—Sifel, Nicolaus & Company—downgraded the stock to "sell" from "hold," suggesting it was overvalued. Analysts at the firm also said Google's growth prospects may be diminishing and that the disappointing earnings results from Yahoo! would force investors to start to more realistically appraise the value of all companies involved in the Internet search and advertising sector. After all that can you guess what happened on the following trading day after Google's big drop? The stock rallied by 7 percent to close at $427.31.

I wonder how many investors sold when Google fell to $440 or $420 a share; or how many people threw in the towel when the stock tanked and hit $399 a share. Now I'm not weighing in at all on the merits of Google as a stock. I am, however, pointing out that even well-loved names on Wall Street can have substantial volatility. Depending on at what point you buy an individual stock, you may risk buying at the top. So rather than worrying about whether you're buying the proper stock (i.e., one that will go up in value) or whether or not that stock has peaked, a far better tactic is to concern yourself with your broader portfolio and make sure that you have the right combination of stocks, bonds, cash, or other investments. Once you determine what's appropriate for you—and let's say it's 60 percent stocks, 30 percent bonds, 5 percent real estate holdings and 5 percent cash—then you also have to monitor that portfolio and make sure that the investments you buy are in line with your desired asset allocation mix. Don't let your investments operate on autopilot and assume that everything will be okay. Over time, your investment objectives or financial needs and goals may change, possibly requiring a change in your asset allocation formula. Also, as you get older, you may become more risk-averse, and you may want a more conservative portfolio, thus necessitating you to amend your asset allocation mix.

Lesson 6: Investing Earlier Is Exponentially More Advantageous than Starting Later

To really optimize your long-term wealth, you need to make wise choices about being a diligent and consistent investor as soon as possible. So many people think, "I can't afford to invest," because of various commitments like paying the mortgage, credit card payments, or other bills. My philosophy is that you can't afford *not* to invest. If you want to achieve millionaire status, don't procrastinate. Don't make excuses about other things that are more pressing. What could be more important than achieving financial security and independence? These things won't happen if you put them off and say, "I'll get to that tomorrow." You also shouldn't wait until you get a large lump sum of money or until you reach a certain age. The earlier you begin saving and investing, the better your chances for building long-term wealth. And if you save more money at an earlier age, you won't be forced to play catch up and sock away large amounts of money during or right before you enter retirement. Savvy investors use an investment strategy called *dollar cost averaging*. This requires you to set aside a fixed sum of money to invest each and every month, no matter how the overall stock market is faring. When the stock market weakens, smart investors see that as a buying opportunity.

> **Savvy investors use an investment strategy called dollar cost averaging.**

DON'T BUY HIGH AND SELL LOW!

Unfortunately, untrained and undisciplined investors stop investing during market dips. They basically adopt a wait-and-see attitude, using the logic that they don't want to invest when the market is down, so they'll resume investing when the market recovers. This is precisely the wrong thing to do because it means that you're always behind the curve. If you wait to see if the market comes back in order to invest, by the time it actually does rebound, you've missed out on that upswing. Moreover, you jump back in and buy when the stock prices are higher. That's exactly the opposite of the buy low and sell high philosophy you've no doubt heard about.

Automatic investments help you become disciplined as an investor.

When you dollar cost average, however, you're able to buy shares at a lower overall cost because you buy on the dips. If you have only a relatively small amount of money to work with, you should still make saving and investing a priority. It's crucial, in fact, in your efforts to become a millionaire. There are companies, such as Sharebuilder.com, where you can invest as little as $25 a month on a regular basis to help you develop consistency and discipline as an investor. Clearly, it'll take you an awfully long time to hit the $1 million mark if you're only investing 25 bucks monthly. And most investors obviously have the ability to contribute far more than that to their portfolios. But the point is to get yourself started doing something—no matter how small. Over time, even small amounts of money can really add up. And investors who've been at it the longest are typically investors who are the wealthiest. Set up an automatic deduction from your paycheck to devote toward your investments each month. That way you won't be tempted to forgo investing if you get panicked about what the financial markets are doing at any given time. Automatic investments also help you become disciplined as an investor.

THE PRICE OF PROCRASTINATION

To realize how powerful and effective it is to save early on, let's assume you want to retire at age 65 and you're now 30 years old. If you invest $10,000 a year in your 401(k) between the ages of 30 and 40, and you earn a 10 percent average annual return, upon retirement you'll have a handsome nest egg that tops $1.7 million.

But what if you wait until age 40 to start? Your 401(k) balance at age 65 will be considerably smaller, just under $700,000. Starting earlier not only provides you more money later in life, because of the magic of time and compounded interest working on your side, but you'll also have less stress about your investments because you won't have to purchase risky investments as you age in order to seek high yields and make up for lost time. And speaking of lost time, starting earlier is a smart idea because over time inflation can—and will—erode the value of your hard-earned dollars.

Again, say you want to save money for retirement. Most experts say you'll need at least 70 to 80 percent of your preretirement income to live comfortably. I think you should plan on needing 90 to 100 percent of your preretirement income because you could live to be 90 or 100. After all, the average person leaving the workforce in 1960 spent just three years in retirement. Now, because of advances in health care and technology, people are living far longer, and retirees today can expect to spend 25 years in retirement. Also, health-care costs are rising dramatically (especially for the elderly), and inflation will always exist—making it more imperative than ever to save a lot and save early.

"Wealthy people have been able to understand and manage their cash flow better. They were disciplined with their savings," says Greg Sullivan of Harris Bank. Sullivan is a former president of the International Association of Financial Planners, the group that merged with the Financial Planning Association in the year 2000 to form the FPA. All of Sullivan's clients at Harris are multimillionaires, and most are completely financially independent. "They're not rich because they found a hot stock," he says. "Even if they were making good money, they were saving their 10 percent or 20 percent a year. They didn't make bad mistakes with the money." Sullivan cites two doctors he knows at the same practice. "One is wealthy, and one is not," he notes. "The difference is that one just lived a simple life, living within his means, and didn't get too fancy with it."

Lesson 7: Fees Do Matter

You should always pay attention to the fees you pay to own various investments. But fees are of particular importance in a flat or down market because fees and commissions can substantially eat into your profits. Earlier I defined what an "expense ratio" is and advised you to stick with no-load mutual funds in order to maximize your chances for investing profits. Well, even with no-load funds, there are hosts of other fees that you should be aware of. Federal regulators at the Securities and Exchange Commission (SEC) generally don't set any limits on the fees that a fund can impose, but the SEC does cap redemption fees at 2 percent in most cases. Additionally, the National Association of Securities Dealers (NASD) does impose some limits on fees. For instance, the NASD says mutual funds must not charge sales loads above 8.5 percent. Despite these restrictions, according to the Securities and Exchange Commission, there are myriad fees you may encounter. Shareholder fees are account fees, exchange fees, purchase fees, redemption fees, and sales loads. With the exception of sales loads, all these fees are charged even on no-load mutual funds. Under annual fund operating expenses are distribution or service fees, also known as 12b-1 marketing fees in the industry; management fees; and other costs, such as custodial, legal, or accounting expenses. As an investor, it's important that you at least know which fees are typical, and which are excessive. When you encounter the latter, especially among funds that haven't performed to your expectations, you're probably better off seeking alternative investments that are better-performing and less costly in terms of fees imposed. I should make a point here, however, about paying fees for advice that you value.

Be willing to pay for service or advice that generates a definite and positive return.

As in all things, you generally get what you pay for. So don't take my admonition to watch out for high mutual fund fees to mean that you should not pay for skilled guidance from a competent investment professional. If someone is clearly helping you to make money, or is contributing value-added wisdom and insights to your investment strategies and financial planning program, then that person is probably worth every penny being charged. In other words, don't be penny-wise and pound-foolish when it comes to being willing to pay for something (in this case, service or advice) that is generating a definite and positive return for you.

Lesson 8: Risk and Reward Go Hand in Hand

Investing in publicly traded securities means taking on risks, any way you look at it. There's the risk of the economy going sour and hurting various industries in which you might invest. There's the risk that the company whose stock you bought may become less competitive and may offer inferior products or services than its rivals. If you invest in bonds, there's interest rate risk. In short, every investor must deal with the fact that when you put your money into the capital markets, there's a chance that you might lose some—if not all—of your investment.

HOW MUCH RISK CAN YOU STAND?

If you have a hearty appetite for risk and can sleep at night even if your investment loses 5 or 10 percent of its value in a day or a week or some other short-term time frame, then you're likely a very risk-tolerant investor. Such investors typically have aggressive growth-oriented stock portfolios, and they seek returns in the 15 percent range and above. If you can stomach some risk, but would like to safeguard a little more of your principal, you might be in the middle-of-the-road camp where investors with a moderate risk profile typically fall. These investors want returns averaging about 8 percent, so their primary holdings consist of a fairly equal mixture of both stocks and bonds. Then there are investors best described as conservative in their orientation. They shy away from risky investments and want to protect their principal at any cost. These investors stick to safe investments, like certificates of deposit (CDs) and government bonds, and they're comfortable seeing their investments grow at a clip of about 4–5 percent a year because at least they can sleep at night without worrying about their investments.

There are a multitude of Web sites and financial services firms out there that will help you assess your own ability to tolerate risk. And frankly, you'll come across a slew of adjectives to describe the individuals or investments that I've just described as aggressive, moderate, or conservative. What is central to all of them, though, is that they seek to help you identify which investments will ultimately make sense for you based your personal comfort level and knowledge of investing, as well as your goals and the time frame for your investing.

DON'T INVEST OUTSIDE YOUR RISK COMFORT ZONE

As an investor, once you realize where you fit in on the risk scale, it's important that you accept what that means. For the aggressive investor, it means that some years your higher-risk investments may not pan out and you may actually lose money. Of course the upside is that you may have certain years when your portfolio significantly outperforms the broader market. As an investor of moderate risk tolerance, that means you can't realistically expect consistent annual returns in the 12 –13 percent range (or higher) without substantially reaching for yield, thereby changing the true mix of your investments toward a more aggressive stance. If you're a conservative investor at heart, don't tell your broker, "I don't want to lose money" but then ask him or her about every hot stock you hear about on CNBC. Accepting these realities is part of understanding the true nature of risk and reward on Wall Street.

The short and simple truth is that when you dial up the risk in your investment portfolio, you have a greater chance for fatter returns—and bigger losses. And when you maintain a relatively low-risk investment strategy, your returns will also be low, and you also take the chance that inflation will outpace your portfolio's investment performance. One of the best places I know of to teach you about risk—and about investing in general—is the National Association of Online Investors (http://www.naoi.org). The NAOI offers a six-course, Internet-based tutorial program called "The Confident Investing Series." It teaches you all the basics you need to know, and then some, about investing on Wall Street. Best of all, the first course in the NAOI's investing series—in which you learn about risk, setting financial goals, how mutual funds work, and how to buy and sell stocks—is free of charge.

FACTORING IN YOUR BROKER'S "BIAS RISK"

Leland Hevner, the president of the NAOI, has an interesting theory about risk in the financial markets. Hevner notes that the vast majority of investing books concentrate on company-specific risk and market risk. "But we break out risk into multiple factors, and we also integrate bias risk." That's the risk that you'll get poor advice or unsuitable recommendations from a broker or financial adviser because, "They often sell you what they make commissions on," Hevner says. But you take that "bias risk" out of the equation when you do your own homework and evaluate your adviser's suggestions, Hevner adds, saying, "The goal of obtaining investing knowledge is to minimize risk. This is not rocket science, even though many in the industry will try to make you think it is." Hevner recommends that when you evaluate an investment, you compare its average performance, risk, and expenses against the performance, risk, and expenses associated with similar investments.

"That will tell you a lot about a potential investment," he says. And speaking of looking at "averages," consider also the wisdom of the CFA's Robert Johnson when it comes to taking on risk. According to

Johnson, investing is not a zero-sum game. "Investing is a positive sum game. And just playing the game, your odds of becoming successful are very high," Johnson asserts. "People think they have to outperform the market averages because it's not a principle that we've grown up with: that being average is okay. Everybody wants to be *better* than average. But 'average' in the investment community is perfectly OK. You can build a great deal of wealth over a long period of time, and you're going to do it without a lot of angst," Johnson adds.

ADVICE FOR THE VERY RISK-AVERSE

What should you do if you're truly risk-averse but you still want to get decent returns? First off, shop around for investments with which you're comfortable. That may mean staying away from stocks and equity mutual funds, until you become more knowledgeable or comfortable in that arena, and sticking with more conservative products like certificates of deposits or money market accounts. Remember, the downside of such conservatism is that, while rates and terms on savings accounts can vary dramatically, they won't get you anywhere near the returns you can get in the capital markets.

Right now the average money market account pays about 2.9 percent. But you can certainly do far better than that—if you know where to look. According to Bankrate.com, institutions like Capital One and UFBDirect.com were offering some of the best rates in the country on money market accounts—about 4 percent—in early 2006. You should also negotiate with your bank or brokerage firm. Most consumers don't realize that they can negotiate for better rates and terms on financial products and services. For instance, you may be able to earn higher rates on your savings and investment accounts based on having multiple accounts with an institution, or based on the combined business your household is giving that bank.

Finally, use a strategy called "laddering." That's where you buy various savings and investment products, each of which has a different time frame attached to it. So let's say you're interested in CDs. You ladder your portfolio by going up the investment scale one rung at a time, buying a CD that matures in one year, another that matures in three years, still another that has a five-year term, and so forth. By laddering, you maximize your return on CDs, and you also have adequate access to your cash.

Lesson 9: Minimizing Mistakes often Results in Maximum Profits

If there's one fact I've learned from interviewing thousands of experts on Wall Street, it's that there is no such thing as a "natural born" investor. Sure, some people may appear to have a "golden touch" and a keen sense of what to invest in for big profits. But even the pros make mistakes; sometimes huge errors. Often, the difference between successful investors and unsuccessful ones can be seen in how each group handles those missteps.

Those of you who read my first book, *Investing Success*, know that investing legend Charles Schwab wrote the foreword to that book, saying: "As Lynnette Khalfani so wisely points out, all investors make mistakes from time to time. But the most successful investors are those who are able to learn from these blunders and make wiser decisions in the future." During an interview, Schwab also told me that he'd made enough mistakes "to fill three books." It was then that I realized that savvy investors like Schwab possessed the unique ability to admit when they'd made a mistake, to correct that mistake, and to move on. This may sound simple, but in practice it is remarkably difficult for most investors to do. Emotions such as fear and greed often cloud our judgment.

THE DIFFERENCE BETWEEN INSTITUTIONAL AND INDIVIDUAL INVESTORS

Rather than admit a mistake, as is the case with a stock or mutual fund that performs poorly year after year, most people would prefer to hang onto those money-losers in the hopes of breaking even. By contrast, institutional investors like mutual funds and pension funds often let go of the dogs in their portfolios far quicker than individuals, or so-called retail investors. And guess what? As a result, institutional investors get nearly triple the return of individual investors, according to Dalbar, a Boston-based research firm. Additionally, individual investors who chase returns—trying to buy into hot funds after those funds have already experienced significant gains—often sell those investments too quickly, or at the wrong time. Investors in equity mutual funds hang onto their investments for just over two years. Data from Dalbar indicate that from 1984 through 2003, the average equity investor earned just 2.57 percent annually, compared to inflation of 3.14 percent and a return of 12.22 percent for the S&P 500 index. Meanwhile, during that 19-year period, the average fixed-income investor earned only 4.24 percent annually, versus returns of 11.7 percent for the long-term government bond index. Clearly, chasing returns and failing to invest for the long run are just two of the mistakes you want to avoid if you want your investments to turn you into a millionaire.

Lesson 10: Process Is More Important than Product

In *Investing Success*, I argued that mastering the investment process is far more important than trying to figure out which specific products (such as stocks or bonds) to buy. My theory was that people who adhered to an investing system—meaning a concrete investing plan, a set of goals, and specific criteria for buying, holding, and selling investments—would naturally become more disciplined investors and would therefore be far more successful in their pursuits. I still believe that it's critical to have an investment process that you follow. And I'm pleased to say that many other experts agree with me.

"Don't start worrying about what stocks you're going to trade, until you set a goal . . . and have a systematic methodology," warns Hevner, of the NAOI. He adds: "You buy and sell when there's a reason to do so in the context of an overall portfolio plan." Based on your unique goals and needs, the NAOI's experts can help you develop an investing process that suits your risk tolerance, as can BetterInvesting (formerly known as the National Association of Investors Corp. or NAIC). BetterInvesting is a nationwide educational organization composed of roughly 200,000 people who are either individual investors or investment club members.

Frankly, I believe you can achieve stellar results using just about any viable investing process—provided it's rooted in some of the tried-and-true wisdom that I've discussed in this chapter. In many cases, one system of investing is really no better than another. What often makes a system work, though, is an investor's willingness and ability to stick to the system. It's only by following the rules and accepting the discipline that an investing process or system requires that you get to take emotion and whim out of the investing equation. As a result, your investing efforts are much more methodical, logical, practical, and profitable.

The Money Coach's Advice for Becoming a Successful Investor

Here is my own unique take on how you can become a successful investor—indeed a millionaire investor. I believe that to invest well, consistently, and over a long period of time, you must master the five-phase process of investing. This five-phase process of investing is defined as follows:

1. Strategizing to meet your own personal goals.
2. Buying the right investments for your individual needs.
3. Holding and monitoring the assets in your portfolio.
4. Selling investments in a judicious manner.
5. Dealing effectively with financial advisers.

CRAFTING A STRATEGY FOR SUCCESS

The strategizing phase of the investing process focuses on setting specific, measurable and realistic goals; developing a prudent asset allocation strategy; and taking care of the financial basics before you invest. Financial basics refer to things like getting rid of debt, establishing a three-month cash cushion, obtaining adequate insurance coverage, and having a will created before you invest. Once you do these things, then you're ready to hit Wall Street. (You'll read more on what types of insurance you need—and don't need—in Chapter 6. And in Chapter 7, you'll learn about the importance of having a will.)

BUY LIKE A PRO—OR HIRE ONE

In the buying phase of the investing process, you have to avoid a number of pitfalls such as relying on tips and inside information as the basis for making purchasing decisions; having concentrated wealth and a lack of diversification; and becoming overconfident in your investing skills. I certainly don't want any investor to feel that he or she can't take control of his or her own financial destiny. But it's a mistake to forgo any outside advice if you could really use it. And I don't mean off-the-cuff advice from your sister or your co-worker in the next cubicle at the office. They probably don't know much more about investing than you do. I'm talking about getting paid advice from a trusted, professional adviser.

Says Johnson of the CFA: "When people are sick, they go to a doctor. When people get into legal difficulties, they see an attorney. But for some reason people think it's a sign of weakness to go for financial help to financial professionals. You should definitely have a working knowledge of investing. But there are still going to be times when you're going to need professional help."

KEEPING A CLOSE EYE ON YOUR INVESTMENTS

Those who master the holding phase of the investing process learn how to monitor their portfolio on a regular basis instead of checking things out haphazardly or letting their investments run on autopilot. During this phase, successful investors also spread their assets out over the proper number of accounts, they rebalance their portfolios as necessary, and they update their investments if their personal circumstances or goals change.

THE IMPORTANCE OF HAVING A SELL DISCIPLINE

The selling phase of the investing process is perhaps the biggest area that trips up investors. When you conquer the selling phase, you learn to take taxes into consideration—but not to make investing decisions based solely on taxes. In the selling phase, it's also critical to create and stick with a sell strategy or a discipline that helps you sell investments in the most judicious manner possible, in a tax efficient way, at the right time, and for the right reason. People who are successful investors also avoid two big selling snafus: missing opportunities to take profits and letting your emotions rule your decision-making process.

The final phase of the investing process is dealing effectively with financial advisers, whether they are accountants, brokers, financial planners, or other money managers.

THE RICH PAY FOR HELP—SHOULD YOU?

Studies show that wealthy people are far more apt to use financial advisers than are people of average means. This makes sense. If you have more money, obviously you want to protect and preserve those assets. But I suspect there's a bit of the chicken and egg syndrome going on here also. It may be correct that the rich have advisers because they can *afford* to pay those advisers. But it is likely also true that many wealthy people got that way *because* they hired help. In other words, they weren't always rich. Rather, they got assistance along the way, and thus they became wealthy. I think that's something you should keep in mind when you contemplate whether or not you can afford to hire qualified financial help.

Again, my theory is that you can't afford *not* to—especially if you're not willing to do the required leg work to manage your own personal finances and figure out what investments are best suited for your needs and objectives. Greg Sullivan, of Harris Bank, says you should make your hiring decision based on specific criteria. "You hire someone for four reasons: time, temperament, talent, and trust." Like Hevner, of the NAOI, Sullivan says that what he does isn't overly complicated rocket science. "I could teach any of my clients to do what I do, but the problem is that most people don't have time. It takes years to learn to manage money well," Sullivan says. At Harris, "We train people for five or six years before they have client work (and manage customer assets). We think it takes that long to really learn about financial planning and investing."

Aside from time, you have to consider your temperament. Can you be dispassionate about your investments? If the market suddenly dropped by 20 percent—or even surged by 20 percent—would you be able to make unemotional, rational, buying and selling decisions? Unfortunately, most people can't. As far as talent is concerned, you should obviously hire someone with experience and a proven track record. If you're a savvy and knowledgeable investor, then by all means run your own show. But if you don't fit that bill, why should you hire yourself, so to speak? And last, the trust factor should loom large in your mind when you're deciding on a financial adviser. Ultimately, you have to feel confident that the individual in question will make decisions in your best interests, and not just to line his or her own pockets.

HOW TO FIND AND HIRE A GOOD FINANCIAL ADVISER

If you do decide that you need help, use some of these ideas to pick a competent professional. Call the Financial Planning Association at (800) 282-7526 or go online to http://www.fpanet.org. The FPA Web site lets you obtain a list of up to 10 certified financial planner professionals in your area. You can also get references for stockbrokers and financial advisers from family and friends you know. Interview at least three prospects before you settle on any adviser. That way you get a sense of different management styles, and you're less likely to have buyer's remorse as a result of not doing your homework.

Ask potential financial planners about their education, professional background, licenses or credentials they hold, whether they operate on a flat-fee or commission basis, how they would describe their typical clients, and how they like to do business—whether through in-person meetings, phone, e-mail or snail mail. Also inquire about how often you can expect to hear from this person. Will the two of you review your financial progress quarterly, annually, or on some other time table? Try to match yourself up with an adviser who seems ethical, experienced, and educated. He or she should also have extensive knowledge of people in the same personal situation you are in, as evidenced by the adviser's client base. For example, if you're a small business owner with very specific financial needs, you'd want a financial planner who serves a lot of other entrepreneurs.

CHECKING AN ADVISER'S BACKGROUND IS A MUST

Also check out the individual with the SEC, with state regulators at the North American Securities Administrators Association, and with the National Association of Securities Dealers (NASD), which operates a central registration depository that provides detailed information about investment advisers, including whether or not they've ever been disciplined or sanctioned by authorities for wrongdoing with their clients. Finally, trust your gut instincts. Go with the person you best click with, you can feel comfortable trusting, and whom you think is the most qualified. Be sure to get the person's ADV, or adviser form, Parts I and II. It makes certain mandatory disclosures about the person's track record and experience. Jon Stokes, senior policy analyst at the CFA Center for Financial Market Integrity, says the relationship between a client and an investment manager is a very intimate one. "You're turning over all kinds of personal information, so choosing the right one can help you avoid picking someone unscrupulous," he says.

Equally important, any adviser you hire should be willing to provide you with pretty much anything you ask—whether it's for client referrals, information about his or her background, or a detailed written explanation about his or her fee structure. "It's very much a relationship based on trust," says Stokes. "Since you're giving them all kinds of information, if they're not willing to do the same, then that's a big red flag that maybe they're someone you don't want to deal with." At the end of the day, if you can master the five phases of the investing process—avoiding the pitfalls inherent in strategizing, buying, holding, and selling investments, as well as dealing with financial advisers—you're well on your way to becoming a millionaire investor.

6

OVERCOME SETBACKS AND MINIMIZE RISKS TO YOUR FINANCIAL HEALTH

It's a sad fact of life that bad things happen to good people. We can't always explain why. We don't know when ill-timed twists of fate will occur. Neither can we predict exactly how a particular calamity— whether a natural disaster, a personal tragedy, or some other problem —might affect us or our families. What is certain, though, is that every day millions of people suffer through a litany of unfortunate events that threaten to undermine their financial well-being.

You might get sick and need an operation—and of course that comes right after your employer shaves your health-care benefits plan, so now the insurance company won't pay your medical expenses. Or maybe your 16-year old daughter gets into a bad car accident, and now you've got huge doctor bills compounded by the fact that you've lost time on the job because you want to be by her bedside. Or even worse, you go into work one morning and at the end of the day your boss hands you and everyone else in the department a pink slip because of poor economic conditions. When you go home to cry the blues to your wife, you find that she's got her bags packed near the front door and—even before you can spill your guts about being laid off—she informs you of more bad news: she's leaving you and wants out of the marriage. For some reason, when we go through difficulties in life, they always seem to come in rapid succession.

I'm not trying to be a "Negative Nellie," I'm just pointing out that when life throws you a curveball, you can often expect a 100-mile-per-hour fastball to come barreling at you right behind it. It's rare that you actually have to deal with just one personal or financial problem at a time. I guess that's why there's a saying that, "Bad news comes in threes."

The Six Dreaded Ds

Many setbacks we face in life also lead to big money challenges. I call these setbacks The Six Dreaded Ds: downsizing, divorce, disability, disease, death in the family, and disaster. If any one of these happens in your family's life, it can quickly throw your finances out of whack—resulting in massive debt, wiped out savings, and even bankruptcy. How can you protect yourself against the Ds or cope with them if they occur? From a financial standpoint, it's very straightforward: you minimize the risks of these misfortunes wreaking havoc in your life. And the best way I know to minimize risk is with insurance. Now, I have good news and bad news.

The bad news is that you'll probably be shocked by the dizzying array of insurance I'm going to advise you that you need. Sorry! But this book couldn't be all fun in the sun. Actually, if you follow my recommendations, you *could* be relaxing in the sun—taking a nice vacation on the beach without worrying about whether you failed to turn off the coffee pot and burned the house down, or didn't lock the front door and gave a burglar access to rob you blind. Either way, you'd be covered.

So, the good news is that insurance, believe it or not, will be a key part of your millionaire asset protection strategy. You don't want to work your rear end off to see everything go up in smoke (literally) because you haven't adequately addressed risks that could have been easily mitigated. And here's even better news: although I'm going to give you the low down on the truckload of insurance you need to help prevent and overcome financial difficulties, I'll also give you the skinny on how to affordably get the coverage you need—as well as tell you which insurance you can forgo because it's largely a waste of money. But let's first start with a quick explanation about why you need any insurance at all.

The Castle and the Moat

As a Millionaire-in-Training, you've got to think of your household— and all the potential threats to it. In medieval times, when leaders at war wanted to outduel their enemies, they set themselves up in elaborate, well-protected, highly fortified castles. To guard against attackers known and unknown, the castle and its king were protected on all fronts. The castle was usually situated on high, rocky ground, on an isolated penin- sula, or on a lake island. The castle's walls were made of stone, spanning up to 40 feet high, and were 7 to 20 feet thick. The foundation, too, was built to withstand the fiercest of attacks—whether they came from enemy troops or Mother Nature's torrential winds and rains. The castle had a drawbridge that could be lifted to keep outside forces from enter- ing at will. And, of course, perched high atop the castle was the tower —usually 100 feet or so off the ground. From this strategic vantage point, the castle's rulers could see potential invaders coming far away. Then there was the moat around the castle. Whether wet or dry, the moat was the flat, open area surrounding the castle, and it was used to slow down the enemy or prevent him from reaching the castle entirely.

You couldn't take cover in the moat because there was no place to hide. Once someone crossed into a dry moat area, he might find himself pummeled by spears. In a wet moat, like a lake, there might be crocodiles, wooden spikes, or sharp objects that would cut down swimmers. Every consideration was given to defending and fortifying the castle against attacks and against the elements.

How Strong Is Your Financial Fortress?

Now consider your own house. Have you built a financial fortress around it? Or are there vulnerable spots where anyone or anything can easily attack you and render you defenseless? Have you established a lookout post—or a plan to see and protect yourself against faraway dangers before they land on your doorstep? Or is your front door weak, your castle full of blind spots that are inviting to enemies like the Ds? If you have proper insurance, that won't be the case. Insurance can be used both defensively and strategically. It can slow down trouble, or make it difficult for problem people or situations to get to you. Therefore, you buy insurance to protect yourself against risks that you're not willing to assume. For example, if you believe that a catastrophe like a major illness would create a severe financial hardship for you, then you need to make sure you have adequate health insurance coverage. If your house is valued at $450,000 and you wouldn't want to spend that amount of money to replace it in the event it was gutted in a fire, then you get homeowner's insurance to offset that risk.

So now that I've hopefully convinced you about the importance of having insurance, let's take a look at the key areas of coverage you can't afford to do without. For most of you, it amounts to life insurance, disability insurance, health insurance, homeowner's insurance, auto insurance, as well as an umbrella liability policy. Some of you may also need long-term care insurance or business liability coverage. We touch briefly on those subjects at the end of this chapter.

Life Is Better with Life Insurance

According to the National Association of Insurance Commissioners, more than 2,000 companies in the United States sell life insurance. While there's no shortage of individuals and entities marketing life insurance, there's a definite shortage in the number of Americans who are adequately protected by this valuable coverage. By industry estimates, more than 25 million Americans—roughly one in five households—don't have life insurance. Among those who do own life insurance, experts say, most are vastly underinsured.

You need life insurance if you fit into any of the following categories: you have minor children; you're married and your spouse relies on your income; you own a business; or the value of your estate exceeds $1 million. How much coverage you need is a question of some debate. Depending on whom you ask, financial planners suggest you get life insurance coverage equal to anywhere from 5 to 10 or even 15 times your annual earnings. This is a rule of thumb that certainly can give you some guidance. So let's say your annual salary is $65,000. Then your life insurance policy should fall within the range of $325,000 to $650,000 or $975,000. Clearly, that's a wide gap. While the latter figure, $975,000, will obviously go a lot further for your heirs, you don't want to overinsure yourself, paying money needlessly for extra life insurance if it's not in your family's best interest. After all, there may be far better ways you could put your money to use instead of spending it on life insurance premiums. So for a more specific determination about your life insurance needs, you really should evaluate your situation based on how much money your family would need to maintain its lifestyle in the event of your death.

Think about several categories of needs your family might face. They will need immediate money to bury you. The average funeral now costs about $10,000. According to the National Funeral Directors Association, as of 2004, the latest date for which information is available, the average funeral cost $6,500. That cost includes an outer burial container, but it does not include cemetery costs, i.e., cemetery lot charges (for digging and the plot of land), expenses for monuments/grave markers, and/or the cost of vaults, not to mention flowers, etc. Thus the $10,000 price tag. Your family may encounter estate taxes and legal fees. Family members might want or need to pay off debts, like credit card bills, auto loans, or mortgages. If your surviving spouse requires help to get retrained to enter the workforce or obtain a degree to get a good or better-paying job, you might consider the cost of education in your life insurance calculation. If your kids will need additional child care because only one parent will be around, factor that into the needs equation as well. Other expenses for the kids you might want to see covered are their educational costs or future college tuition. (The total price tag to attend a private university for four years now tops $100,000. If you have a child age eight or younger, double that cost to account for tuition inflation over the next decade.) And last, if you want to ensure long-term financial stability for your spouse in your absence, you should consider whether or not you want to provide a nest egg for your partner that provides him or her with a supplemental stream of income for a fixed period of time, or for the rest of that person's life.

Some of you may view that as excessive, figuring, "Hey, if I die, my spouse had better get a job—or get remarried!" Others of you though, for your own personal reasons, may want to provide that extra financial security when you're not around. Obviously, you can see that the numbers can add up fast.

To quickly calculate your estimated life insurance needs, go to http://www.prudential.com. Click on Prudential's "Financial Planning" tab, and then use the "Life Insurance Quick Estimator" that is found under the section called Planning Tools and Guides. Ultimately, you have to pick a policy with a face value that you feel comfortably meets your needs, and that you can afford. For instance, a policy with a $500,000 face value means that upon your death, your beneficiaries will receive $500,000 from your insurer.

The Insurance Information Institute says that in 2006 the annual premium for a 40-year-old male purchasing a $500,000 20-year level term life insurance policy will be $641 if he qualifies as a "standard" risk. His life insurance rate is cheaper, $352, if he meets the more stringent requirements of a "preferred" risk. Rates for women would be even lower. A big benefit of purchasing life insurance is that if you die, the proceeds don't go through probate, a lengthy court process in which your will has to be "proven." Instead, life insurance proceeds pass by beneficiary designation, meaning that whoever is listed as the beneficiary on the policy will get the money without having those funds tied up in court.

TERM LIFE INSURANCE

Term insurance covers you for a specific period of time.

You have two basic options for the types of life insurance that are available to you: term insurance and permanent insurance. Term insurance, as the name implies, covers you for a specific term, say 20 years. Term insurance is the most affordable type of life insurance you can buy, and it can provide you with sufficient coverage to protect your family and give you peace of mind, especially if you have minor children to consider.

A woman who is a nonsmoker in reasonably good health can currently get a $1 million term policy for around $500 annually. I think that's a very small price to pay to safeguard your family's interests in the event you're not around. When you explore the universe of permanent insurance options that are available, you'll find that the policies get a lot more complex and a lot more expensive. That isn't to suggest, however, that you shouldn't look into this type of insurance. If cash flow is an issue, start by purchasing a term policy to make sure that you have immediate coverage. Later, when you can afford permanent insurance, consider adding that to the mix.

PERMANENT LIFE INSURANCE

Permanent life insurance, also called *whole life insurance*, lasts your entire life and the premiums you pay are fixed. Part of the premium you pay is invested, giving you funds that build up on a tax-deferred basis. You can borrow from a permanent life insurance policy. And if you die owning a permanent life insurance policy with cash value in it, your beneficiaries receive both the face value of the policy and the cash value that has accumulated.

That same 40-year-old nonsmoking woman in good health can get a $500,000 permanent life insurance policy for roughly $3,000 per year. Again, prices can vary wildly, so do shop around. Be sure that you understand the guarantees contained in your policy, as well as any charges or "surrender penalties" you may get hit with if you choose to drop the policy. Life insurance can help you pass on assets in your estate without incurring estate taxes. So consider these facts if you do purchase large amounts of insurance.

Permanent life insurance lasts your entire life, and the premiums are fixed.

If you die anytime between 2006 and 2008, you can leave up to $2 million to your heirs tax free. That figure jumps to $3.5 million in 2009. Federal estate taxes, also known as inheritance taxes, top out at 46 percent in 2006, and 45 percent in the years 2007 through 2009. Estate taxes are supposed to be repealed entirely in 2010, meaning the estate tax rate goes to 0 percent. But if Congress does nothing, the estate tax rate will go back to 55 percent in 2011, and the amount of money you can transfer tax free to your heirs falls back down to $1 million.

Protect Your Income Stream with Disability Coverage

Statistics from the Health Insurance Association of America show that if you are between the ages of 30 and 55, your chances of suffering a disability are three to five times greater than your odds of dying. In fact, in the United States, 56,700 people become disabled every day, the National Safety Council reports. This means that every two seconds, someone becomes disabled! Moreover, the average short-term disability lasts for 64 days, and the typical long-term disability lasts for 31 months (or two-and-a-half years), according to the U.S. Group Disability Rate Study & Risk Management Survey by JHA Inc. Disabilities happen because of mishaps at home, motor vehicle crashes on the road, and various accidents on the job, to name a few causes. While the reasons behind personal disabilities may vary, what all disabilities have in common is:

- They can happen to anyone.
- They prevent you from working—thus cutting off your income stream.

You have to look at your ability to earn a living as an asset. If that asset gets diminished because of an accident or illness that results in a disability, your family's financial health is greatly impaired. Therefore, the purpose of having disability insurance is to protect (i.e., replace) your income in the event that you fall victim to a disabling injury or illness.

DISABILITY COVERAGE ON THE JOB ISN'T ENOUGH

Most of you probably know whether or not you have disability coverage through your job. For those of you with this insurance, I'm guessing that many don't know *exactly* how much disability insurance you have. It's also likely that you are unfamiliar with the conditions that must be met in order to have that coverage kick in. After all, very few people spend their lunch hours or their free time poring over insurance documents. But possessing enough coverage, and having a policy that is flexible enough to benefit you if necessary, is an important part of protecting your personal finances.

Disability insurance you obtain through work is not portable, so if you lose your job, quit, or your company closes, the insurance vanishes.

Make it a point to read through your benefits package, or ask a human resources professional at work for guidance to learn about the specific disability insurance coverage you have. How soon does it pay your benefits after your first day of missed work resulting from a disability—after the thirtieth or sixtieth day you're off the job or some other time? In many cases, disability protection through your employer's plan covers only 60 percent of your salary. Imagine that. Many of you have a hard time getting by on 100 percent of your paycheck. Think of how severely you'd feel that crimp in your budget or in your lifestyle if you had to get by on just 60 percent of your take-home pay. What's more, do you realize that company-paid disability payments are fully taxable? Ouch. That 60 percent payment gets slashed further by Uncle Sam dipping into your pocket. Finally, disability insurance you obtain at work is not portable. In other words, if you lose your job, quit, or your company folds, that insurance vanishes.

MAKING DISABILITY INSURANCE AFFORDABLE

If you are the sole breadwinner in your family, disability insurance is especially vital. But even in two-income households, if your partner or your children rely on your income, disability coverage is important. For individual disability coverage, the average cost of an annual policy is $1,277, according to LIMRA International. To lower your costs, start by buying a supplemental disability insurance policy that will add to any existing coverage you may have from work. It's much easier and far less expensive to get disability coverage when you are employed versus unemployed or self-employed. So getting another policy now means that if you ever sever ties with your employer for any reason, at least you'd still have disability coverage. And here's another reason to get supplemental coverage. The National Safety Council says that two out of three disabilities occur off the job, and aren't covered by workers' compensation.

When you buy a policy, keep it affordable by selecting a longer elimination period. This refers to the period of time between the date your disability begins and the time you are eligible for benefits. So let's say you get a disability policy with a 30-day elimination period. This means that your insurer will begin making payments to you 30 days after you first suffer a disability and can't work. A policy with a 90-day elimination period is common, and will be cheaper than a policy that requires your insurer to begin kicking out payments to you 30 or 60 days after you become disabled. Also, picking a shorter length of time that the insurer must pay you can also keep those disability premiums down. If you don't have disability insurance at work, see if you can get coverage through your memberships with groups or organizations to which you belong. As with all things, shop around for the best deals available. This is a definitely an area where putting in a little extra time and effort could pay off for years to come.

The Hazards of Not Having Health Insurance

Even if you have health insurance on the job, don't assume that it would pull you through any medical crisis. For many Americans, a major illness or a lengthy hospital stay often results in financial ruin because most health insurance plans won't cover all the medical costs you'll face. As a result, a study by researchers at Harvard University has found that nearly 50 percent of the people who file for bankruptcy protection in the United States do so because of big medical bills. Of those bankruptcy filers, 75 percent of the people actually had health insurance when their illness began. Still, "even middle-class, insured families often fall prey to financial catastrophe when sick," the study noted. Rising health-care costs for employers mean that more companies are putting the burden of increased health-care premiums on their workers.

Businesses get employees to shoulder the high cost of health care by raising plan deductibles, increasing the amount of co-pays you must make at doctor's visits, slashing coverage, and switching their offerings from HMOs (cheaper health maintenance organizations) to more expensive PPO (preferred provider organization) medical plans.

> **An HSA is similar to a 401(k) account, except that instead of saving for retirement, you're putting money away to cover future medical expenses.**

If you don't have health insurance through your employer, you're not alone. An estimated 45 million Americans currently lack basic health-care coverage. Those without this vital insurance are especially vulnerable to financial problems stemming from serious—and expensive—illnesses. And please don't think, "It couldn't happen to me or my family." Every year, 10 to 15 percent of Americans are hospitalized, according to the Kaiser Commission.

HEALTH SAVINGS ACCOUNTS BECOME POPULAR

Despite the gravity of the situation, there are some things you can do to get health-care insurance—or get it at cheaper rates than you might be currently paying. For starters, set up a health savings account, or HSA. These are relatively new vehicles that allow you to save for health-care related needs on a pretax basis. An HSA is essentially a checking account that's linked to a health insurance plan. An HSA is similar to a 401(k) account, except that instead of saving for retirement, you're putting money away to cover future medical expenses. Health savings accounts made their debut back in 2003, when only a handful of firms offered them.

Today, nearly 500 banks and financial institutions—including Bank of America, J. P. Morgan Chase, and Fidelity Investments—offer these accounts. By 2010, roughly 10 percent of all those insured in the United States—more than 15 million Americans—will have an HSA, according to projections from DiamondCluster International, a management consulting firm. Right now 3 million Americans have HSAs, with an average account balance of $1,500.

Here's how an HSA works. You must set up a high-deductible health plan—meaning one with a deductible that's $1,000 or more for individuals or $2,000 or higher for families. You contribute before-tax dollars to the account and take out funds on an as-needed basis to cover your medical, vision, and dental expenses. The amount you save gets rolled over from year to year. If you can afford to raise your deductible a bit, you can save money on the monthly premiums. To open a plan, you have to be under the age of 65. For 2006, the tax-free contribution limit to an HSA plan was $2,700 for individuals and $5,450 for families, or the amount of their deductible if it is less. But look for the government to raise the tax-deductible contribution limits to encourage consumers to put more money into HSAs—a proposal backed by President George W. Bush. Finally, unlike traditional health plans offered by employers, your health savings account belongs to you, so you can take the assets in it with you even if you change jobs. The money you don't immediately use can be invested in stocks, bonds, and mutual funds and it grows tax-free. Provided you later spend the funds on health-care expenses, the money never gets taxed. After you turn 65, you can withdraw any money left over without penalty, but you will pay taxes on your withdrawals.

PROTECTING YOURSELF AGAINST A MAJOR ILLNESS

Buying a critical-illness policy can also be used as a stopgap measure until you can obtain more comprehensive and more affordable health-care insurance. With a critical-illness policy, you pay a set monthly premium. If you get stricken by cancer, a heart attack, stroke, or some other major illness, you're given a lump sum to utilize any way you choose, instead of having payments go to your medical-care providers. Enduring a serious injury or chronic illness is devastating enough. Don't compound that tragedy by going without health insurance. A medical crisis can quickly strip you of your hard-earned assets, putting a severe dent in your quest to become a millionaire.

WHAT TO LOOK FOR IN THE FINE PRINT

To optimize your health-care benefits, know what's covered in your policy and what's excluded.

Look at the benefits section of your health plan and pay attention to the areas that outline your emergency benefits, hospital and extended care benefits, medical and surgical benefits, mental conditions/substance abuse benefits, and prescription drug benefits. Make sure you have a policy that does, in fact, cover your actual and/or anticipated needs. If you don't, switch to one that does. Next, examine the "exclusions" section of your health-care policy to get a firm grasp of what coverage isn't being provided. Keep a close eye out for any sections with the heading "Limitations" or "Definitions." These areas will tell you exactly what restrictions exist and to what extent they may affect your health-care coverage. Also, maintain up-to-date health-care records. You'll need detailed information about the people you spoke to, the treatment you received, or the bills you were sent in the event of a dispute with a medical provider, or in the event you have a health-care claim that your insurer denies. Since information is power, always document everything. Additionally, investigate what rights you may have outside of your existing health plan.

STATE LAW MAY OFFER MANDATORY COVERAGE

Believe it or not, many health-care rights are mandated by state law and may supersede what's in your policy, health-care attorneys say.

For example, while there is great variance in terms of exact rules and provisions, every state has so-called "mandatory benefits" laws. That's why most states require benefits for what are known as "mainstream health issues" like pregnancy and childbirth. Furthermore, states nationwide have adopted a patchwork of health-care mandates that may benefit you. Do you live in Maryland? Residents there get mandatory coverage for Alzheimer's disease. Or perhaps you reside in Alabama. That means you qualify for health-care benefits for sickle cell anemia. Meanwhile, the states of New Jersey and Virginia have mandated coverage for those afflicted with hemophilia. As you can see, knowing your own state's mandatory benefits laws could help you tremendously if you suffer from a chronic illness or if you have an insurance claim that is wrongfully denied.

HOW TO GET UNFAIR HEALTH CLAIM DENIALS REVERSED

If your medical bills aren't covered by your health insurance but you learn that your condition is supposed to be covered as mandated by your state's laws, write down the statute number and quote it chapter and verse to your insurer. If it still balks, and denies your claim, insist on a written explanation for the denial. Be diligent in your record-keeping in all your conversations, and then take your grievance to your state insurance commissioner, state Department of Health, and attorney general's office. By becoming an activist when it comes to your health care and by using the law, you can often get unfair denials reversed.

What else should you do if you are denied a medical claim or you're frustrated by the health-care system? You might also hire a medical advocate to work on your behalf. For $15 a month for individuals or $25 monthly for families, companies like New Orleans-based Patient Care (http://www.patientcare4u.com) will help you navigate your way through the health-care industry, file claims, or report grievances you have about your health-care coverage. If your employer offers Patient Care's services, you can get an advocate for an even cheaper price— around $2 to $5 a month. Other companies offering similar services can be found on the Web on in your local telephone book. Just be sure to check references and investigate any company you consider through the Better Business Bureau.

Help with Your Homeowner's Insurance

As of 2006, the average cost of homeowner's insurance nationwide was just under $700. The Insurance Information Institute reports that, in recent years, the average price of homeowner's insurance has risen by between 3 and 5 percent annually. Such price increases seem to be here to stay because of a number of factors: the increasing prevalence of natural disasters such as hurricanes, floods, earthquakes, and tornados; big jumps in housing construction costs; and the emergence of mold as a major factor in insurance claims and insurance lawsuits. Despite the risks of any number of disasters, experts believe that 45 million homes in the United States—nearly two out of three residences—are underinsured because homeowners aren't carrying enough property insurance to cover the cost of replacing their homes in the event of catastrophic damage. Some people simply don't want to pay more for insurance. Others, however, don't understand how much coverage they truly need. Generally speaking, you should buy enough homeowner's coverage to insure your home for 100 percent of its value, including your possessions inside the house.

STICK TO REPLACEMENT COST POLICIES

Look for what's called a *replacement cost homeowner's policy*. Don't buy a so-called cash value homeowner's policy. With a replacement cost policy, if your house was wiped out by a fire or hurricane and it would cost, say, $350,000 to rebuild it from the ground up, then that's the amount of insurance you should have. With a replacement cost policy, your insurer won't pay you less than what it would take to rebuild your home, regardless of the age or current value of your house.

By contrast, you may be paid less than what it would take to rebuild your home with a cash value policy. Sure, a cash value policy is cheaper. But if you have a massive loss, you may not be able to completely replace damaged property because your insurer will reimburse you only for the value of what your house and the contents inside were worth at the time of the loss. In other words, the insurer will pay you what you originally paid for the house and its contents—minus depreciation for age, wear, and tear. Most homeowner's policies with 100 percent replacement cost usually include anywhere from $100,000 and $300,000 in liability coverage. But if your net worth is more than that, you should get larger amounts of coverage to safeguard yourself from lawsuits or to protect your home, which may be your largest financial asset.

If you rent, you should get renter's insurance to protect your valuables. According to a poll conducted by the Independent Insurance Agents & Brokers of America, 64 percent of people living in rental properties don't have insurance. That's a mistake, especially given the very affordable cost of renter's insurance—around $150 to $300 per year. Renter's policies usually cover $30,000 to $35,000 worth of personal property and offer $100,000 to $300,000 worth of liability coverage.

INSURING VALUABLES AND COLLECTIBLES

Your homeowner's policy may not cover or may impose a cap on coverage for items like rare coins or paintings, expensive china, furs, jewelry, or collectibles. If you own any of these, ask your insurance agent about a "floater" to adequately cover them. You may first have to get an appraisal to determine the current market value of such precious goods. But if you treasure these valuables, it's probably worth the effort and expense of an appraisal. To ratchet down the cost of homeowner's insurance, start by raising your deductible to save money on your premiums. For example, going from a $500 deductible to a $1,000 deductible often shaves 25 percent or so off your annual homeowner's insurance costs. As mentioned earlier, maintaining stellar credit can also go a long way toward controlling your insurance expenses.

THINK SAFETY FOR BIG SAVINGS

In general, you'll achieve the most savings on your homeowner's insurance bill by doing everything you can do to make your home safer, thereby decreasing the likelihood of some kind of disaster or accident taking place. For instance, putting in a smoke detector can usually knock at least 5 percent off your insurance bill. Even better, if you don't smoke—or if you stop smoking—advise your insurer of this because you'll probably get a discount. Insurers figure that the risk of a fire caused by careless smoking is greatly diminished in households that do not have smokers.

Theft deterrents such as burglar alarms or dead-bolt locks also often qualify for insurance discounts.

But before you start making major home-security upgrades—such as putting in an expensive sprinkler system or installing a sophisticated fire and burglar alarm unit that signals the police or fire department—contact your insurer to ask whether these systems actually qualify for a discount. If you feel that you need them for your family's well-being, fine. But don't get them solely to save money on insurance without weighing the trade-offs between the cost of the system and the insurance discount it will provide. You can also install modern electrical, heating, and plumbing systems in your home—all of which decrease the risk of fire. Then let your insurer know about these systems in order to get a price break for making these upgrades. If you're in an area of the country that's prone to storm damage, getting storm shutters or installing a sturdier roof could also save you big bucks with your insurer. Both of these will also add to the value of your home, should you later sell.

Squeezing Every Possible Discount Out of Your Insurer

You've heard of multiple-car discounts, when two people in the family own vehicles that are insured by the same company, right? Well, you can also get a discount in the range of 5 to 15 percent when you buy your auto policy from the same insurer that provides your homeowner's coverage. Further discounts are possible if you buy life insurance with the same insurer. Don't nickel and dime your insurance company to get reimbursed for every little loss you incur. Placing small claims can make your rates go way up—or may even make you a candidate to get canceled by your insurer.

Finally, shop around to get the latest, most competitive insurance rates. Services like InsureMe.com (http://www.insureme.com) promise to provide you with up to five free quotes from agents eager to compete for your business. Other helpful Web sites for comparison shopping include www.accuquote.com, www.insweb.com, www.insurance.com, and www.quotesmith.com. When you get a couple of quotes, be sure to look into the background of any insurance company you consider. To check out an insurer's reputation—after all, you don't want to choose a company that might not be around in 10 or 20 years if you ever do file a substantial claim—inquire about the company through the Better Business Bureau, which maintains records about customer complaints; your state Department of Insurance, which licenses and sanctions insurers; and A. M. Best, which can tell you about the financial strength of an insurer.

Less Costly Car Insurance

Auto insurance rates vary widely from state to state, neighborhood to neighborhood, and household to household. As anyone with a teenager in the house can attest, in some cases the price for auto insurance coverage can be absolutely ridiculous. Obviously, your driving history determines a lot of your insurance rates, but how much you'll pay for car insurance also depends on your credit, your age and experience as a driver, the type of car you own, the incidence of crime in your city, and other factors.

The Insurance Information Institute says that the average American driver spends about $700 a year on car insurance. However, the National Association of Insurance Commissioners (NAIC) puts the average price tag for auto insurance at $880. But again, rates are all over the place. In New Jersey, the most expensive state in the nation as far as car insurance goes, typical drivers fork over $1,284 annually to cover their vehicle.

Meanwhile in Iowa, the most affordable state for insurance, drivers pay an average of just $638 to cover their cars, according to the NAIC. To keep your insurance rates as reasonable as possible, maintain a clean driving record, avoiding tickets, accidents, and aggressive driving at all costs. You can take a driver's safety course to lower your car insurance premiums, maintain moderate amounts of coverage, raise your deductible, opt for vehicles with safety features such as air bags, install antitheft devices, or buy a less expensive car that is cheaper to repair, and therefore cheaper to insure. As with homeowner's insurance, you have plenty of options when it comes to buying auto insurance.

Again, the Internet is a great tool for comparison shopping, so start there. Also ask friends and family about insurers they use—especially if they are satisfied with their rates, coverage, and service. You won't really know if you're getting a good deal, however, until you get at least three quotes. So make sure you get competing bids for your business.

Go with an insurer with a good reputation and financial stability that offers good coverage at a price you can afford.

Umbrella Liability Insurance

You're at a higher risk of getting sued if you're a high-profile individual, if you own a dog, have a pool, drive a lot or have a teenage driver, often have personal guests or workers at your home, or own a business. All these instances expose you to big liabilities and risks that can be lessened by having a personal umbrella policy.

Personal umbrella policies extend your household protection, covering claims above and beyond what might be paid via your homeowner's or auto insurance policy.

An umbrella liability insurance policy covers you for claims above and beyond what might be paid via your homeowner's or auto insurance policy. In essence, personal umbrella policies extend your household protection. Standard limits for umbrella policies fall in the $1 million range, but you can get far more coverage, up to $10 million or so, depending on your specific needs. You should also get an umbrella liability policy if you have large amounts of cash, real estate investments, or otherwise easily identifiable assets you'd like to protect—especially in this litigious society.

If someone slips on your sidewalk, if your dog bites a neighbor, or if your child's playmate breaks a bone while playing in your backyard, you could easily be subject to costly lawsuits and potential liabilities. Many people will think nothing of suing you in court for $100,000, $500,000, or more for these kinds of mishaps. If you do get sued in such a case and someone wins a judgment against you, that umbrella liability policy will kick in to pay off what the court says you owe.

Personal umbrella liability policies pay out in excess of the limits of your homeowner's insurance. So if someone gets a $1 million verdict against you and your homeowner's policy has a $300,000 cap, then an additional $700,000 would be paid by your umbrella policy. Personal umbrella policies are relatively cheap, usually around $200 or $300 a year. Yet, they offer a very solid extra layer of protection to guard you and your family against potential financial disaster. I strongly recommend that you add this coverage to your homeowner's insurance.

It's fast and simple to do. Just call your insurance company and tell the representative that you want to add this important coverage. Think about an umbrella policy as your way of escaping a 20-year prison term. Let's say you're 40 years old. You get sued, and you lose everything you've built over the years. That's like sentencing yourself to a 20-year prison term because that's easily how long it might take you to replace a lifetime of assets squandered just because you didn't fork over $250 a year.

Insurance You Can Skip

While it may seem that you have to spend an exorbitant amount of your budget on all manner of insurance, you'll be pleased to know that there are several forms of insurance to which you can say, "Thanks, but no thanks." The first is hospital indemnity insurance. It's cheap—typically only a couple hundred dollars annually—but it provides you with only limited coverage. Most policies pay just $100 per day for your hospital bills. That's peanuts when you consider that it actually costs 12 times that amount, about $1,200 daily, for the typical hospital stay. Extended warranty insurance is also usually unnecessary. If you go into an electronics store or a retailer that sells big-ticket items like refrigerators or washers and dryers, a salesperson may try to offer you extended contract insurance. Don't go for it. The cost is too high relative to the value you may get out of it. If that new $900 treadmill you buy suddenly breaks down three years after you buy it, you would have already spent nearly a third of that amount in insurance. But by that time, the same treadmill will be far cheaper than it is today—if they still make that model. Chances are there'll be a newer, far superior model that you will want later. And after spending days or months trying to get your insurance company to fix or replace your existing treadmill, you'll get some refurbished model that will probably break down again in another year or two. In my opinion, the same thing applies to cell phone insurance and insurance for most electronic gadgets. Besides, when you buy these things with a credit card, the credit card company often extends the manufacturer's warranty.

Specific health policies are another money-waster when it comes to insurance. These are the policies that protect you when you get specifically covered illnesses or diseases, like cancer. Unfortunately, this type of insurance is just far too narrow in scope and contains too many exclusions. You're far better off getting a broader, more comprehensive health insurance policy that would cover you no matter what might befall you.

I also don't recommend life insurance for your children. Remember: the purpose of life insurance is to replace the lost income of someone who is supporting a family. Does your child contribute financially to your household so that you rely on his or her income? If the answer is no, then don't buy life insurance on that child. Some agents will try to sell you on life insurance for children under the rationale that if your child dies, you would at least have coverage to pay for burial costs. While it's true that funerals are expensive these days, the chances of a young child dying are far lower than the risk of an adult passing away. Moreover, if you've been following all the steps I've outlined throughout *The Money Coach's Guide To Your First Million*, you should have more than enough assets to deal with this kind of financial emergency—in the remote chance that such an unfortunate death does occur.

Last, don't bother with flight insurance. You (or your heirs) reap benefits from this type of insurance only if you get terribly injured in some specifically designated way or if you die. Just like the odds of a kid dying, your chances of being killed in a plane crash are very remote. For those of you who travel a lot, or travel on the spur of the moment, don't confuse flight insurance coverage with trip interruption or travel cancellation insurance. Every once in a while, it may pay to have that type of insurance if you're booking tentative plans, business trips, or vacations that you think may not pan out.

Who Needs Long-Term Care Insurance?

Generally speaking, you don't need to worry about getting long-term care insurance until you are in your fifties; buying it sooner than that is really unnecessary for most people. After that point, though, it's very important to have. If you've been paying disability coverage year in and year out, think of your long-term policy as a sort of continuation of that coverage when you move beyond your working years. Long-term care coverage protects you if you get sick in your old age and require skilled nursing care at home or you need to enter a nursing home facility. Depending on where you live, nursing homes can run an astounding rate. According to the MetLife Market Survey of Nursing Home and Home Care Costs, a private room in a nursing home costs, on average, $70,080 per year, or $192 per day. The typical stay in a nursing home is 2.4 years, bringing the total cost to $168,192. It's a scary thought to consider that being in a nursing home for just two years—perhaps because of a chronic illness or some debilitating condition—could wipe out a big chunk of your life savings. To avoid this catastrophe, you can buy an individual long-term care policy from an insurance broker, or get long-term care coverage through a group or association to which you belong. Be warned though, it's not cheap. People in their fifties pay more than $1,000 a year for long-term care coverage, according to Bankrate.com. And a senior citizen aged 65 in relatively good health can expect to shell out between $2,000 and $3,000 annually for a long-term care policy, the AARP says. For additional information, log onto the NAIC's Web site at http://www.naic.org, and order a free copy of its "Shopper's Guide to Long-Term Care Insurance."

Lighting a Fire Under You

Look, this may be the least exciting chapter in this book from your perspective. All this talk about insurance might be the kind of stuff you ignore. After all, smokers ignore cancer warnings on cigarette packs, and alcoholics ignore conventional wisdom about the dangers of excessive drinking too. However, this is truly one of the most important chapters in *The Money Coach's Guide to Your First Million*. Every day, scores of people get sick, die, or become disabled. And each day, courthouses nationwide are filled with folks slapped with lawsuits—from celebrities to unknowns. Do yourself a favor: go visit your local courthouse. You have the right to do so as a citizen. Sit in and listen to some of the cases presented—everything from failed marriages to business deals gone sour to claims about destroyed property. This is not the glamorous stuff that you see on Court TV. That stuff doesn't generate any ratings. But trust me: the majority of cases are just like the ones I just described.

And, if you've got two nickels to rub together, let alone a million dollars, as far as some people are concerned, you're a perfect target to become their next meal ticket. If you don't have time to get to court, read the tabloids, and, if that doesn't convince you, examine the public notice section of your local newspaper. All the foreclosures you see aren't just from families who can no longer afford their mortgages. Those repossessions don't just stem solely from deadbeat bachelors wheeling around town in BMWs on McDonald's salaries. And all those estate liquidations aren't just the result of the deaths of someone's great Aunt Sally or Uncle Jasper. What quite possibly happened, in a majority of these cases, is that people spent too much time enjoying the best of times, without spending enough time preparing for the worst of times.

Don't let this be your fate.

7

NEVER FORGET THE
NEXT GENERATION

When my daughter Alexis was born in November 2005, I wasn't quite prepared for how fussy a baby she would be. Every day she would go through crying spells—yelling her head off, turning beet red, and generally having a fit. I tried everything: nursing and burping her, rocking and walking her, playing with her, or changing her diaper. But nothing seemed to work. Her father would coo and cuddle with her, carry Alexis around in an infant carrier, or give her warm baths—all with little effect when Alexis was in one of her sour moods. Mind you, I'm not a first-time mother. I already have two children. My first daughter, Aziza, was a pretty easy baby, and my son, Jakada, was moderately fussy when he was a newborn. But after six weeks or so, he settled down. Alexis Cheyenne, however, was so fiercely independent that we created a unique nickname for her. In public, Alexis was a complete doll around others; often quiet as a church mouse and full of smiles. People would take one look at her adorable face and say, "What a sweet little princess." In return, we'd smile and say: "Yes, we call her 'the warrior princess.'" Then we would explain that this beautiful angel of ours also had quite a set of lungs on her. At times her screaming got so bad that her dad would put on these huge ear muffs —I'm talking the heavy duty kind worn by construction workers operating jackhammers—because Alexis's shrieks pierced his eardrums.

Great Grandma's Wisdom

One day when Alexis was about two months old, and I was weary, tired, and sleep-deprived in that foggy-headed way that only new parents and torture victims can truly understand, Alexis's great grandmother called, wanting to know how everything was going. I told her the truth—that Alexis was as precious as could be, but that she'd also turned our household upside down with her feisty temperament. Nana, who was 86 years old, listened carefully and then simply said: "You treat her right, Lynnette." "Oh, of course, Nana, I will. I love her," I answered. And then, as if I didn't get the full meaning of her statement, Nana repeated: "Treat her right and be nice to her, Lynnette." Then she added, "Don't forget: she'll be the one picking out your nursing home." When I heard that advice, I just cracked up laughing. Amid my laughter, I realized that Nana was joking—mostly. But there was a grain of truth to her comments as well. I'll never forget Nana's wisdom. And if you have children, or plan to in the future, neither should you. The underlying message to Nana's wise counsel is this: the way you treat your kids can come back on you—for good or ill.

Creating a Culture of Stewardship

As parents, we don't often reflect on how the ways in which we handle our kids might affect them—or us—down the road. That's what this chapter is all about. If you have a goal of becoming a millionaire, an important part of that mission has to be thinking about the next generation. I'm not suggesting that you treat your children well and think about your heirs just so that they'll take care of you in old age. Rather, I want to stress how long-lasting, generational wealth is sustained only by proper financial planning and creating a culture of stewardship that will last for years and years to come. By doing so, you will leave a wonderful financial legacy for your children, and even their children's offspring too.

What would you like to be known for generations from now? How would you like to be remembered by your family and friends? Many of us want to be great role models for our children and generous benefactors to our heirs. Wouldn't it be nice to know that upon your death you can pass on millions of dollars that would benefit those you love most? To create a financial legacy that you can be proud of, however, you have to do more than simply leave money to your heirs. You have to do as Nana urged me to do with Alexis: treat them right. As your Money Coach, I'm going to tell how to treat your family right financially, while preserving and passing along wealth in the best possible manner—and creating the least amount of family stress and chaos. These strategies can be summed up based on four areas of your life:

1. The *example* you set for your children.
2. The *attitude* you convey toward money.
3. The *environment* you allow your heirs to experience.
4. The *assets* you leave behind upon your death.

Let's look at each of these areas separately.

Setting a Positive Example

Bob Sullivan is a millionaire many times over. He owns his own business, has two homes, and lives a very comfortable lifestyle. He's also tried to teach his children, ages 20, 17, and 13, about being good stewards of their money. The number one lesson, he says, is to instruct your heirs about spending wisely. "I've never seen a level of income or net worth that can not be outspent," he says. "People can make a million bucks a year and still have credit card debt."

Living within your means is still the key to financial stability.

Sullivan should know. He's also a certified financial planner and a partner at Sullivan & Serwitz in Los Altos, CA. According to Sullivan, a lot of the behaviors that people young and old engage in stem from the "cultural garbage" embedded in our society. He contends that the marketing machine on Madison Avenue works overtime each day to send you the message that you need to "buy, buy, buy" in order to be happy. But, "Living within your means is still the key to financial stability," Sullivan says. "It's always been that way and always will be. Even people who have millions of dollars are not exempt from that law." If your actions don't show your children this basic truth, then you're not setting a good example for them to be proper stewards of their money—no matter how much or how little they may have.

A Case of Do as I Say, Not as I Do

Let's face it. A lot of us don't set the best of examples when it comes to teaching our kids about how to handle money. In our hearts and minds we want to be good role models, but in practice we often fall short of where we'd like to be. I'll be the first person to admit that I've made many mistakes in modeling the behavior that I want my children to emulate. I remember the time when my son was about four years old and he got into an "I want this," "I want that phase." Initially, it baffled me, because I really thought I was doing a good job of teaching my kids about limits and that they would not always get everything in life that they wanted—especially just because they saw some toy in the store or some commercial on the television.

But one day, when Jakada was experiencing a case of the "gimmes"—you know, "Mommy, gimme this" and "Mommy gimme that"—I sat down and reflected on my own actions and analyzed why it might be that he seemed to want so much stuff. It didn't take me long to realize that I, in fact, had contributed to his bad case of the gimmes. After all, since he was in preschool weekdays and I was working full-time, it was only on the weekends that Jakada would spend eight straight hours or more with me. And what did we do during that time? When there weren't playdates, parties, or extracurricular classes to attend, our family ran around doing all the errands that couldn't get done during the work week—shopping for groceries, dropping off laundry, getting the kids clothes or shoes, and so forth.

Aligning What You Say with What You Do

So despite my telling him about being careful with money and how we handle it, Jakada took away the idea that money is to be used only to buy stuff—apparently the more stuff, the better. I believe he also got the idea that our time was best spent out shopping or doing things that actually required us to spend money. I had unwittingly set an example of excessive consumption for my children.

Clearly, this was not the message I wanted to convey. It was around that time that I came across a four-chambered piggy bank. Instead of the traditional piggy bank, which has just one slot in it, this one had four openings into which children could insert coins and dollar bills. The four slots are labeled: "Save," "Spend," "Invest," and "Donate." The idea behind the bank, which I later discovered was called the Money Savvy Pig, is to teach kids that there are four things that you can do with money, not just one (spending). When I got this bank, I immediately had an "aha!" moment. I knew it would be very helpful in showing my son—and his older sister Aziza—that they have choices with money and that they should consciously think about what they do with their money. Both of my children immediately "got it" when I gave them each a Money Savvy Pig and explained the concept behind it. They even understood about investing when I described it to them in age-appropriate terms.

Alexis is still an infant, less than a year old, and hasn't yet been introduced to her own piggy bank. But my two older children, who are now 8 and 6, still love their Money Savvy Pigs. Aziza has most of her money put away in the "Invest" portion of the bank, which is covered by a sticker of a graduation cap. "I'm investing for college," she told me. Meanwhile, Jakada gets excited whenever he puts money into the "Donate" section of his pig. Recently, after he put a sticker of a globe on his Money Savvy Pig, I asked Jakada why he did that. "I want to help the homeless people of the world," he replied. Needless to say that warmed my heart and made me feel like I was doing something right as a parent. "Money can be an empowerment tool if you infuse it with stewardship and philanthropy early on," says Susan Beacham, founder of The Money Savvy Generation, the company that created the Money Savvy Pig.

Using Common Activities as Teaching Moments

No matter whether your children are 2, 12, 20, or 45 years old, each of us teaches our children something about money by the example we set. Even if you don't have kids of your own, have you considered the possibility that, by your behavior, you could be setting an example for the young people around you—your nieces or nephews, the neighborhood kids, and so on?

Evaluate your purchases out loud to your children.

For those of you with young children, it's imperative that you use everyday experiences to teach them practical money management lessons. You don't have to be a financial expert to do this.

Just think about your usual weekday or weekend routine with the kids and capture those "teaching moments" that naturally occur. When you're out food shopping, for example, do you walk down the aisles of supermarkets and recklessly throw whatever comes to mind in your shopping cart? I can picture some of you now. As your cart fills up to the brink, when you can't possibly cram any more items in there—at least not without risking a serious spill—only then do you announce to the kids: "Whew! I'm tired and all shopped out. Let's go." Or do you take the time to evaluate your purchases and then say out loud to your children, "I think this is over-priced. The sign says it's on sale. But let me check the unit price of this." Do you take time to explain wise shopping choices to your children, and do you let them know that your family has a budget and that you want to stay within that budget?

Play a game with your young children when you're out on those weekend shopping expeditions. Tell your kids that you want to spend only a certain amount—and then stick to that limit. I guarantee you, your kids will actually have fun trying to help you purchase what you need and stay within the guidelines of that budget. At an early age, kids love rules. They want and need boundaries. And when you tell them up front what they can and cannot do, they'll respond to that positively, rather than seeing it as something restrictive or negative.

Why Young Children Love Rules and Limits

When children learn entirely new concepts, they often equate rules with fairness. That's why, if you teach seven-year-olds to play checkers and explain that they can move their pieces only in a straight line (except for jumping) and one space at a time, they'll go along with those limits pretty much without question. If you further reveal how they can jump the opponent, take one of the opponent's pieces, or get crowned by maneuvering to the back row of the checkerboard, they'll follow those rules too. But the minute you do something outside the rules—say moving a piece laterally or trying to get a crown without being in the right position—they'll definitely challenge you, saying, "You can't do that. That's not fair!"

And they're right. In their mind, the rules dictate what can and should be done, and any deviations from those limits make the game arbitrary and unfair. Children also like rules because they reinforce basic feelings of security for them. When their mother or father (or both) lay down the rules, children innately know the parents are in charge. That's how it should be. Kids want to experience the comfort of having their parents serve as caretakers, the ones responsible for the family's well-being and the basic rules that govern individual and family behavior. When you change the rules on a child, he or she can feel as though things have been turned upside down. That's unsettling and shocking to a child's sense of order and wellness.

Be a Parent, Not a "Friend" to Your Teenagers

Treat your children right by teaching them right. If you're in a financial predicament, don't have bill collectors calling your house or allow excessive stress in your life because of money woes. Kids are mighty perceptive, and they pick up on these things, despite what you may think. On the flip side, if your family has considerable means, you don't have to satisfy your child's every whim. "I just want my children to be happy," or, "I want my kids to have it better than I did." Well, of course you do. That's only natural as a parent. But you can cross the line and move into dangerous territory if you're not careful and you spoil your kids just to make up for what you had or didn't have in your childhood. I also hear many adults, especially the parents of teenagers, say: "I want my child to be able to talk to me about anything."

Having a running dialogue with your kid is definitely advisable.

Again, of course, you do. We all want to keep the lines of communication open with our children. As they get older, they'll face peer pressure, relationship issues, and more. So having a running dialogue with your kid is definitely advisable. But don't make the mistake of trying to be your child's best friend. You're the parent first and foremost. Parents set limits. Friends don't. Parents have the perspective and experience that only comes with age. Friends don't. Parents are legally and morally responsible for their children. Friends aren't. So you'll set yourself and your child up for problems down the road if you try to be anything other than a good and loving parent.

That's not to say that you have to become a child's concept of a "dream mother" or a "dream father" either. I know it feels good when your child says, "You're the best Mom ever!" But let's be real: kids often say that when you give them their own way, letting them have or do something they want!

Parents set limits. Friends don't.

Teaching Personal Sacrifice and Delayed Gratification

When your teenage daughter begs for that $150 pair of jeans, don't simply whip out that platinum Visa card and say, "Here, honey." After all, this is not a TV commercial. This is real life. Talk to her first—and really listen. Let her explain why those jeans are so important in her mind. If it's just because "Everyone has them," be prepared to explain that your household doesn't operate according to everyone else's rules. Otherwise, plan to dole out money the rest of your child's teen years on all manner of things that "everyone has" or for what "everyone does." If you feel she's rationalizing things, ask why that $150 price tag is justified when she easily can get a perfectly nice pair of jeans for a third of the price. If those jeans don't fit into your budget or if you think the price is excessive, learn to say no—and mean it. At the very least, teach your daughter that high-priced items come at a sacrifice.

So, if she really, desperately wants those jeans, maybe she has to make a sacrifice by saving up her own allowance to get them. This is a great way to reinforce the idea of delayed gratification.

Or maybe the sacrifice for getting those $150 to-die-for jeans is that she doesn't get those DVDs and video games she's been asking for. You might also tie her behavior to her ability to get "extra" things from you. And I'm not talking about her getting good grades. That should be expected anyway. I'm also not talking about her following your normal family rules, like coming home on time or keeping her room clean. Again, children should have to conform to your limits without the enticement of some reward or financial benefit. I'm referring to her going the extra mile—or doing something you think is worthy of a bonus, so to speak. That varies from family to family. You may find her mentoring or teaching a younger sibling, totally unsolicited, and want to reward her for that. Or perhaps she takes it upon herself to do additional chores at home. It's up to you to determine what is above and beyond the call of duty in your household.

Encourage Adult Children To Be Responsible

Some financial experts say that children—even adult children—generally have unrealistically optimistic views of their parents' wealth. Perhaps you've given or loaned your children money all their lives whenever they've asked. Just think about what happens when you constantly give big cash gifts to your heirs. Those adult children or grandchildren will begin to depend on this money as part of their own income. It's a shame to see a 40- or 50-year-old adult who has to constantly be "bailed out" by his or her parents because that adult child can't run his or her own financial affairs responsibly.

If you're using money as a tool to control your children, consider this: After you're gone, your children will still relate to money the same way. They'll naturally gravitate toward someone else who will take your place, in terms of exercising control over their lives with money. Is that the outcome you want for your child? I don't think so. Watch out for using money as a way to satisfy your own emotional agenda. In some wealthy households, second-generation kids get turned off by their family's wealth. They've seen the ways in which money has controlled their parents' lives. Consequently, these children sometimes want nothing to do with the money that a parent may try to leave as an inheritance. Even though they could be aided by it, the children simply don't want to be controlled by the money.

Speaking of control, there is one thing you should do to exercise control over assets you may have spent a lifetime building. It's making a will. In the event of your death, that last will and testament is your way of telling everyone how you want your assets to be distributed and who should take care of any minor children you may have. If you think it's important to have a will—and of course, it is—set the right example for your adult children by creating your own will. Most of you need a will —even if you're not rich or elderly. Yet, experts estimate that seven out of 10 adults in the U.S. don't have a will. That's a big financial mistake. If you die without a will, the courts in your state decide what happens with your assets – however large or small they may be. The courts can also determine who should take custody of any minor children you have. And the courts' decisions may be contrary to your wishes. Creating a will doesn't have to break your budget. An attorney can help you draw up a basic will for as little as $250 to $500. The price depends on where you live and the complexity of your situation. A cheaper option is to create a will online. At www.legal-zoom.com, you can create a standard will and testament for $59. Also, www.Buildawill.com offers basic wills online for just $20. If you do use an Internet company, after you create your will, be sure to get it notarized and signed by at least two witnesses.

Examine Your Attitude Toward Money

What's your own attitude toward money? Do you view it as a means to an end? Or do you view it as the end itself? Your children, whether youngsters or adults, definitely pick up on your attitude toward money; and they will consciously or unconsciously adopt those attitudes, or outright reject them. Good money management is holistic. Avoid going to extremes. Don't make your children feel as if money is the ultimate source of satisfaction or the sole route to happiness in life. Similarly, don't convey the attitude that you don't care about money and that it's totally unimportant. Neither attitude represents truth or reality. In your approach to money, you don't want to be overly permissive or cavalier, nor do you want be a miser when it comes to finances. You want to instill in your children a great work ethic—especially if your family has tons of money.

Cultivate a healthy attitude about the subject of personal finances.

We all want our children to appreciate the things they have, to understand the value of a dollar, and to not take for granted that money will just always be there for them. You also don't want your children to think that, if they constantly mismanage their finances, you will always come to the rescue. Don't be nonchalant about the power and impact of money. Additionally, don't be secretive about what your family has or doesn't have; that makes money a taboo subject in your household, which is damaging. Cultivate a healthy attitude about the subject of personal finances. That attitude, in turn, will help your children respect money and the fact that they must work in order to obtain money.

Unless things change radically in this country, most people won't be exposed to any kind of formal personal financial training, education, or curriculum. The lucky ones will get some classes when they're in high school or perhaps even college. But that's late in the game. So their first experiences with money and the attitudes they associate with it are primarily learned at home. It's no wonder that so many young adults find themselves deep in financial ruin in their late twenties and early thirties, less than 10 years after entering the job market, when most get their first taste of handling large sums of money. For some, the "real world" is too overwhelming and too expensive. They wind up living under their parents' roof, sometimes creating a long-lasting cycle of dependency.

Seeing the World Through Your Child's Eyes

Have you ever looked at the world through your children's eyes? Take a minute now and analyze the environment in which your children live on a regular basis. Think about where they spend most of their time and with whom. For some individuals, it's mostly at school or with neighborhood friends. For others, it might be on the job or in civic activities. When your children are at school, work, or just hanging out with the neighbors, what economic conditions do they see? Is everyone around them well off—or does it at least appear that way? Do they spend most of their free time at the mall, in front of a television full of commercials, or someplace else that's designed to get people to spend money? Or are your children surrounded by relative poverty and people who seem to be struggling financially?

All these environments influence children in a profound way. As a parent, it's up to you to control—and in some instances limit—the environment in which your children will live and operate. It's my belief that you should expose your children to a wide range of cultures and socioeconomic conditions so that they'll be well-rounded individuals and won't have a lopsided view of the world. Therefore, if you live in the country—on a farm or in some other rural setting—consider taking time to expose your children to life in an urban setting as well. If you live in the inner city, show your child that the world is bigger than that neighborhood alone; ditto for those of you who live in a fancy gated community or a community with homes located on culs-de-sac.

While you're showing your children different environments, talk to them about the economic implications of what they're seeing. Privileged, financially well off children should know that they are fortunate to have the comforts of material wealth. And families that aren't affluent should show their children "how the other half lives" in a realistic way. The idea isn't to say, "Look at what they have; don't you want it?" Rather, you want to convey that material success in life is often tied to hard work and personal achievement. Whether wealthy, poor, or something in between, all parents should explain to children that money doesn't buy happiness. Instead the message should be that having money and being financially stable can help you achieve certain goals in life, whether it's paying for college, starting a business, or donating to one's favorite charity.

Creating a Balanced Environment

Think about your family's lifestyle, too. If it's too stuffy, change it sometimes to loosen things up a bit. Dinner out with the family doesn't have to happen on a Saturday night in a big restaurant with valet parking. It might be going to a local pizza shop where you sit at the counter and have the Friday night $2-a-slice pizza special. Sure, the holidays can be spent watching the tree lighting at Rockefeller Center; but they can also be spent at a local outreach center sponsored by a church, mosque, or synagogue. On Thanksgiving, for example, let your children learn about being truly thankful by arranging for them to volunteer in a soup kitchen, hospital, or homeless shelter. Make them appreciate also the gifts that you give them by not going overboard with presents.

This past Christmas, my kids received a few toys—which came from the local arts and crafts store. And guess what? They really appreciated bead-making kits, simple ink stamps with block letters, and other craft-related items as opposed to the standard toy of the season that crowds of people lined up for, 30 deep, at the nearby Toys 'R Us. My point is to create a lifestyle and environment that reflect the values you want to impart to your children. You've also got to remember that you're the parent, not the child. So don't be a doormat. Your children will take advantage of you if you act like you're an ATM or a slot machine. The kids know: pull Mommy's arm, and the money comes spilling out—just like a Vegas slot machine. If you're what I call a "pushover parent" —the kind that has a tendency to say no at first but then relents—your children soon learn: Pull that arm long enough or protest loudly enough, and Mom will eventually give in and give me what I want. That's ridiculous. With youngsters, you have to show by your actions that there is no room for negotiation when it comes down to who is steering the financial ship for your family. The earlier you get this message across, the easier it will be when they're older.

> **Create a lifestyle and environment that reflect the values you want to impart to your children.**

The Absentee Parent Syndrome

While you're thinking honestly about your kids' environment, ask yourself this: Am I a big part of their environment, or am I practically nonexistent? We all get busy. We all frequently feel overworked. We're tired from the demands of family, career, and civic responsibilities. Consequently, many of us indulge our children with things rather than spending time with them. That's time that could be spent teaching solid financial values—or just simply enjoying life together. So don't use money as a substitute for good parenting. Some parents may not intentionally indulge their kids' every desire, yet subconsciously they believe that children are meant to be seen and not heard. Or perhaps the parents want to avoid conflict. Either way, the result is the same: you buy your children "stuff" in order to keep them quiet.

Make your children see the connection between how wages and money are tied to hard work.

It's in your children's best interests to learn (as early as possible) that they can't have everything they want and that they can't have it all now. If you're a middle-class family, chances are you think other people's kids are the ones with silver spoons in their mouths. I can assure you that someone else looking at your family thinks you're the ones that are well off. Moreover, if you give your son everything he wants—like a cell phone with unlimited use, a state-of-the-art computer in his room, and a car at age 16—don't be baffled later on when he feels a sense of entitlement. Don't set your children up to fail in life by allowing them to be lax about achievement. Make them see the connection between how wages and money are tied to hard work. Nothing is free in life, and they'll need to be equipped to make hard decisions later on in life. So teach them the basics now—about living within their means, saving, budgeting, buying insurance, as well as how checking and savings accounts operate. After all, it's far more effective to *mold* proper financial behavior at an early age than to *change* your child's poor money habits later on.

Passing on Your Assets

Susan Beacham recalls when her eight-year-old daughter Amanda was putting money into her piggy bank. It was right after Amanda's grandfather had undergone quadruple bypass surgery. Amanda took a blank sticker and put a heart on it, then put that sticker on the Donate section of her Money Savvy Pig. She told her mother she wanted to help out financially, just in case "Grandpa Georgie gets sick" again. Amanda—bless her generous heart—ultimately donated the money to the American Heart Association. "Children, they're instinctual givers. In their wonderful way, they think they can solve all problems," her mother notes. "Young children get the power of stewardship because they have a very simple view of life, and donating is very simple."

Placing Your Assets in Trust

The clients who work with Bob Sullivan, the California-based CFP professional, must have at least $3 million in assets to invest; many have substantially more than that minimum threshold. According to Sullivan, there is no better way to pass on money to your heirs than via a trust. "I'm a very big fan of the use of trusts," he says. "Estate planning at a basic level is about tax planning." Currently, couples can pass $4 million tax-free to their heirs. As Sullivan explains, estate planning is really a proxy for you if you're not here. It's your road map for how you want the resources generated by your efforts to be enjoyed by your heirs.

Maybe you want the money spent on education, given to your favorite neighborhood kid, whatever. When you create a trust, how your assets will be spent is entirely up to you. There are a slew of trust options, everything from charitable remainder trusts to so-called QPRTs and GRITs. A QPRT, or qualified personal residence trust, freezes your home at its current value and allows you to transfer any future appreciation to your heirs free of gift and estate taxes. A GRIT, or grantor retained income trust, is an effective estate-planning device if you want to leave money to more distant relatives—not to spouses, children, and grandchildren but to nieces, nephews, and cousins. This trust is commonly used by unmarried partners or same-sex couples to make sure the other is provided for.

But the type of trust that may be of most benefit to the largest number of people is called a *dynastic trust*. Instead of other trusts in which a child turns a certain age and a big lump sum of money gets dropped into his or her lap, a dynastic trust let's you set flexible provisions for when and how your heirs get money. Discretionary income can be given to your beneficiaries any time you want. This can be a more effective way, Sullivan says, to help get the concept of stewardship into estate planning. "People want to talk about how they're going to beat the tax man. But we want to talk about who they are as people or a family." For instance, do you want to leave your children money for a down payment for their first home? A trust can provide for that. Or maybe you'd like to help your kids start a business. If so, a dynastic trust can buy stock in the company. In one trust within Sullivan's own family, his wife specified that if any of their children wanted to open a business using funds from the trust, that child had to first have at least three years' experience in the field.

This kind of trust creates a framework and a structure to help you define your goals for the family and give you the tools to implement your wishes. A trust is also a much better way to keep your assets exempt from creditor claims. It offers very strong asset protection to keep money in the family because trusts keep money secure from bankruptcy, litigation, the claws of creditors, and divorce—all major conflicts that could arise in your family down the road.

The downside to setting up a trust is that it can be somewhat expensive, depending on your circumstances. When you start talking about leaving money to your heirs, what you want to transfer, what you don't want to transfer, and under what conditions your heirs will or won't get money, it gets really complicated really fast. So this isn't something you can undertake on your own. You'll definitely need to get help from a team of professionals who specialize in the area of estate planning, taxes, and trusts. A trust company has to be involved.

But lots of independent trust companies will handle all the legal and tax paperwork, and having a team of advisers needn't be overly costly or especially challenging.

You have to make sure all accounts are titled properly. But the biggest caveat for creating really good trusts, Sullivan says, is to make sure that they're flexible and truly appropriate for your family's needs. For instance, Sullivan says he always likes to see a "change of venue" clause included in trust documents. The thinking is: you might be in California, Texas, or Michigan right now, but what if you later move to another state with different laws, and you die there? Once you die, the trust becomes irrevocable. So Sullivan says that, in his mind, "It's tantamount to malpractice" for any trust expert to create a trust for you without having a change of venue clause.

The trust must also be responsive to the real-life needs of your heirs. Let's say you have four children. In many cases, it can be foolish to simply say, "I'll give them each 25 percent of my assets." What if one of them is a highly paid investment banker and really doesn't want or need the money? What if one of your children has a learning or medical disability that may require expert care for the rest of his or her life? Or what if one child is simply terrible at handling money? All these instances happen all too often. So think through what your family will really need in your absence and make sure your trust documents reflect the realities of your family's unique circumstances. Don't just go to an attorney and have him or her crank out a quick fix—which is a boilerplate document that doesn't best serve your interests.

A Lifetime of Wealth and Generational Prosperity, Too

Consider carefully what you leave to your children and how they might handle a big windfall of money. Experts at Lincoln Financial predict that the number of millionaires in the United States will triple by the year 2013, primarily because of inheritances. If you follow the millionaire success formula that I've outlined in *The Money Coach's Guide To Your First Million*, not only will *you* become affluent beyond your wildest dreams —but your heirs will also enjoy the benefits of wealth, prosperity, and financial harmony for generations to come.

Here's wishing you personal happiness, financial success, and all the blessings you deserve!

INDEX